The Civic Spectacle

THE CIVIC SPECTACLE

Essays on Drama and Community

Mera J. Flaumenhaft

ROWMAN & LITTLEFIELD PUBLISHERS, INC.

ROWMAN & LITTLEFIELD PUBLISHERS, INC.
Published in the United States of America
by Rowman & Littlefield Publishers, Inc.
4720 Boston Way, Lanham, Maryland 20706

3 Henrietta Street
London WC2E 8LU, England

British Cataloging in Publication Information Available

Library of Congress Cataloging-in-Publication Data

Flaumenhaft, Mera J.
The civic spectacle : essays on drama and community / Mera J. Flaumenhaft.
p.   cm.
The first three essays are revisions of essays originally published, respectively, in Interpretation (fall 1989), the St. John's review (spring 1984), and Interpretation (May 1978).
Includes bibliographical references and index.
Contents: Seeing justice done : Aeschylus's Oresteia—Looking together in Athens : Euripides's Bacchae and the Festival of Dionysus—The comic remedy in private spectacle : Machiavelli's Mandragola—Three views of Henry V : Shakespeare, Olivier, and Branagh.
1. Drama—History and criticism.   2. Theater—Political aspects.
3. Literature and society.   4. Politics and literature.   5. Theater and society.   I. Title.
PN1643.F53 1994 809.2—dc20 94-6311 CIP

ISBN 978-0-8476-7964-5

Printed in the United States of America

To the
memory of my parents
Ruth G. Oxenhorn
and
Joseph M. Oxenhorn

Contents

Acknowledgments

My work on *Mandragola* was first made possible by a grant from the National Endowment for the Humanities. This led to my translation of that play, as well as to an earlier version of the third chapter of this book, which appeared as "The Comic Remedy: Machiavelli's *Mandragola*," *Interpretation* (May, 1978), pp. 33–74. Earlier versions of two other chapters appeared as "Looking Together in Athens: The Dionysian Tragedy and Festival," *The St. John's Review* (Spring, 1984), pp. 48–59, and as "Seeing Justice Done: Aeschylus's *Oresteia*," *Interpretation* (Fall, 1989), pp. 69–109. I am grateful to the publishers for permission to reprint.

On several occasions, the interest of Mary Nichols in my work has hastened it along the path to publication. I am grateful for her generosity. Kathryn Kinzer of St. John's College in Annapolis, Maryland, has been most helpful in locating materials I have needed for this study. Only she knows how literally I have taken that old sign, "Have a question? Ask your librarian."

To Leon Kass and Amy A. Kass I owe decades of interest, encouragement, and conversation about the subjects of this book and related matters. Jan Blits and Kathleen Blits have been invaluable in their supply of good advice, editorial suggestions, and helpful comments. Daniel Flaumenhaft has always been a fount of information and a ready sounding board for questions having to do with communities and their public buildings. I am grateful to Benjamin Flaumenhaft for his quick and accurate typing service, for teaching me to cope with the computer, and for advice on punctuation and military history.

My husband, Harvey Flaumenhaft, has been my constant companion—at plays, at the movies, and throughout the writing of this long-term project. At every stage, his questions and suggestions have improved my thinking. There is no one with whom I would rather "look together."

Introduction

This book about the plays and polities of other times and other places is also meant to be a *self*-exploration, a meditation on what we twentieth-century citizens can learn from the plays we watch and the ways we watch them.

Each chapter examines a dramatic masterpiece written at a critical moment in Western civilization and asks what sort of viewing characterizes that moment and what sort of community of citizen-spectators is formed by the looking together that they do in the theater. Each of the plays chosen for discussion is formed from material that is part of the shared consciousness of its audience; the plots are all taken from well-known myths or histories. In each case, echoes and revisions of earlier versions suggest the author's aims in presenting the story anew. By reshaping a story held in common, each author reshapes the community for which he writes. Chapters 1 and 2 consider the formation of the classical city and the danger of its dissolution, and both explore the role of classical tragedy in maintaining such a city. Chapter 3 discusses a modern comedy that aims to subvert and transform the principles of classical politics. Chapter 4 is about the role of a modern history play in forming and maintaining the modern nation-state for which it was written. Each chapter contains an extended close reading of a tragedy, comedy, or history, followed by a discussion of the moral and political effects of both the play and its production. Each also explores how the presentation of political themes *within* the drama is related to the playwright's view of the broadly political function of the theater in his society.

Western politics and Western drama arose at the same time in Athens. These words are Greek, as is most of our fundamental vocabulary for discussing politics and the theater. The theater in Athens was

1

intended to educate, as well as to entertain, the public. It is appropriate that the first two chapters of this book are about Greek plays: Aeschylus's *Oresteia* and Euripides' *Bacchae*. The tragic playwrights explore the tension between political health in the city and persisting human needs and desires that necessarily threaten or subvert civic stability. Both playwrights suggest that neither the city nor the human beings who live in it can thrive unless some safe arrangements are made to supplement orderly, enlightened city ways with the dark ways that are the themes of tragedy. In the first and foremost drama of the Western world, as well as in the last of the greatest Greek tragedies, the story of another, very different city—Argos or Thebes—becomes part of the experience of Athens. This assimilation was accomplished under the auspices of Dionysus, the presiding divinity of the theater; and the entire city was required to watch it.

Centuries later, in a city not very far from Athens, Machiavelli deliberately set out to undermine the political and moral principles that arose in the ancient world. In addition to writing political treatises and a history of his city, the prime founder of modern politics wrote plays—not tragedies, but comedies—the most successful of which he called *Mandragola*. The subject matter of the comedy is private—it is a story of marriage and adultery—but the laughter about these private subjects shares the intent of the teachings about public matters that inform Machiavelli's political writings. Unlike the Greek tragedies, Machiavelli's comedy was seen by small audiences in select private showings. Nevertheless, it was designed to have a powerful influence on the thinking of the influential young men who enjoyed it as entertainment and then went out to govern their cities.

Shakespeare, the prime entertainer and educator of the English-speaking world, wrote not only tragedies and comedies, but histories. He presented his own preeminent prince in the figure of King Henry V, whom audiences have long recognized as the embodiment of at least some version of Machiavellian *virtù*. The London audiences who voluntarily paid to see his plays were smaller than the Athenian citizenry who were required to attend the festival and performances in the theater of Dionysus, but they were larger and more public than those present at performances of Machiavelli's plays. For these audiences, living under a monarchy in a modern, commercial nation-state, Shakespeare fashioned the story of their own recent past. We in our democratic times have seen vast transformations in politics and in other spheres of life. New technology and the demands of a "mass" audience that cannot be contained in one place at one time have produced a new form of public entertainment. In this century, it is possible to see not only new and evanescent productions in the live theater, but also durable products in the movies. Two film versions of Shakespeare's original *Henry V*, separated by forty years, invite us once again to reflect on the relationship between what a community watches as its public entertainment and how it views itself as a community.

Chapter 1, "Seeing Justice Done: Aeschylus's *Oresteia*," is about a city's establishment of institutions of public justice. The first two parts of this chapter focus on the first two plays of the trilogy, discussing kinship and revenge in communities where the primary institution is the family; the last two deal with the development of full civic institutions. The chapter's first part, on the *Agamemnon*, explores the inadequacies of private justice in communities where outsiders have almost no visual access into the affairs of private households, and have little power to act on what little they can see. The second part of the chapter shows that, in the *Libation Bearers*, Argos is still a city in which justice is executed from within the family. But the middle play opens up a passageway between the restricted views and cyclical revenge of *Agamemnon* and the full view and conclusive justice promised in the *Eumenides*. Again the discussion focuses on what is visible and on who is watching. The chapter's third part, on the *Eumenides*, describes the genesis in Athens of fully visible public law in a community of citizens fully on view to each other. Looking at our own institutions of justice—courts, juries, televised trials, plea bargaining, prisons, and executions—the chapter's fourth part asks what we can learn from the dark old ways of Argos, as well as from the enlightened innovations of Athens. Finally, the discussion returns to the theater, the festival, and the city in which the *Oresteia* was originally performed.

Chapter 2, "Looking Together in Athens: Euripides' *Bacchae* and the Festival of Dionysus," gives further consideration to the Greek tragic drama. The chapter's first part, "The Dionysian Tragedy at Thebes," is a reading of the *Bacchae*. It examines Euripides' depiction of the arrival of the Dionysian rites at Thebes, and of the threat they pose to the stable political life defended by the young king who governs there. The chapter's second part, "Tragedy and the City Dionysia at Athens," describes the annual festival in which Athens made Dionysus and what he stood for the object of serious public viewing in the city. The chapter asks what the theater and Dionysus have to do with each other: why would a city that ordinarily keeps this god at a distance think it necessary to look upon him regularly and why should this communal looking be done by spectators in a theater?

Chapter 3, "The Comic Remedy in Private Spectacle: Machiavelli's *Mandragola*," asks why an eminent political theorist would repeatedly turn his attention to the comic theater; it considers the relationship between his comic masterwork and his revolutionary political treatises. While *The Prince* and the *Discourses* present the new teachings as they apply to public affairs, *Mandragola* shows them at work in a private affair. The chapter's first two parts examine Machiavellian *virtù* in the light of ancient and Christian virtue, through a discussion of Machiavelli's attitude toward chastity. The chapter's third part, "Comedy and the Young," explores the relationship between morality and the comic theater, comparing Machiavelli's subversive aims with the aims of Roman comedy and of the Italian *Commedia Erudita*, both of which have long been recognized as superficial models for *Mandragola*. The comparison includes a discussion of the contexts in which these plays were seen, of where they were produced and of who was seeing them. The chapter concludes that Machiavelli's seductive comedy about seduction was very much a part of his broader political project.

Chapter 4, "Three Views of *Henry V:* Shakespeare, Olivier, and Branagh," is an interpretation of Shakespeare's play and of two fine film versions of it that differ greatly from each other. The first three parts compare the two movies almost scene-by-scene. They examine Shakespeare's political themes—nationhood, kingship, leadership, and friendship—as they are presented in the play itself. Editing and additions by the two actor-directors, and the handling of the Prologue, costumes, sets, camera, and music are shown to be responsible for versions of the story which differ both from each other and from the original play. The fourth part of this chapter, "Public Entertainment: The Wooden O and the Movies," returns to the Prologue to *Henry V,* in which Shakespeare depicts Henry as a consummate speaker and actor, and calls attention to the limitations of his theater (the "wooden O") as a realistic imitation of life. It then discusses some ways in which our modern film technology transcends the limitations Shakespeare refers to. Olivier's political motive for making his version in 1944 is compared with Branagh's psychological emphasis, his more internalized view for a less-dangerous and more private time. The discussion raises questions about our own political communities and our own entertainment, suggesting that there are good reasons to hope that we shall continue—at least some of the time—to look together at live productions of plays in something like Shakespeare's wooden O.

It should be acknowledged at the outset that the views which inform this book differ from those now found among some writers about Greek tragedy and those prevalent among writers about the Renaissance and Shakespeare. The chapters are not essays in literary theory or literary history. It is true that I am interested in the context in which plays are read and especially in which they are performed, and I am aware that plays, insofar as they are performed, must, in some sense, be collaborative efforts of authors, directors, actors, and audiences. But I do believe that writers—including writers of plays—have intentions and that thoughtful readers and audiences naturally want to know what they might be. Our theater audiences, moviegoers, newspaper reviewers, and especially our students respond naturally to discussions about people and politics—discussions about good and bad leadership, right and wrong, human nature, and men and women. These are primary concerns—and they should be. The more that literary theory and abstractions about "theatricality" and "textuality" and "sexuality" are prematurely substituted for such primary experience, the less that the books we read and the plays we see will have to do with how we live and what we think about. So I am interested in the "performative event" and the contexts of "playtexts" because I want to think about what sorts of human beings and communities are associated with different arrangements for the production and watching of plays. And I want to do this in the ordinary language that we use when we think about the primary questions in our real lives.

Finally, although this book deals with now-fashionable subjects, such as carnival, rites of passage, and the margins and undersides of normally sanctioned political life, my intention is not to unlink the great chain of being, or to empower the oppressed. Aeschylus, Euripides, Machiavelli, and Shakespeare are rich and subtle thinkers. They are for all times not because they can be enlisted on one side or another, but because they move us and unsettle us and make us think harder about who we are and what we ought to be, whatever the side on which we may find ourselves.

Note on Translations

Quotations from the *Oresteia* are mostly from Richmond Lattimore's translation (University of Chicago Press, 1953), in which line numbers closely follow the Greek text. Translations that differ from Lattimore's are my own. Translations from the *Bacchae* are my own. All Greek is transliterated. I have, in some places, departed from conventional transliteration so that readers who do not know any Greek will be able to appreciate plays on words and to recognize the Greek roots of important English words. Translations from *Mandragola* are from my translation of the play (Waveland Press, Inc., Prospect Heights, Ill., 1981). References to Shakespeare's histories are to *The Signet Classic Shakespeare* edited by Sylvan Barnet (New York and Toronto).

1

Seeing Justice Done

Aeschylus's *Oresteia*

No one knows for sure when human beings first sat together to watch their fellows stage a play. And no one knows when formal trials became regular events in the lives of civilized communities. There is no evidence that these institutions developed together. But watching trials seems to have much in common with watching plays. In both, speech, action, and props are arranged to display events that are not really occurring as they are watched. And in both, a staged representation imitates past or possible events, and elicits the passions and judgments of the assembled spectators. Perennial interest in accounts of dramatic trials, the continual popularity of courtroom dramas and movies, and recent interest in televised trials all suggest that dramatic reenactment and judicial judgment are fundamentally related to each other.

Perhaps it is no accident that the first and foremost drama of the Western world is about the establishment of institutional public justice. Presented in a city where the same citizens are required at different times to constitute themselves as collective spectator in the theater and collective jury in a court of law, the *Oresteia* is at once a poetic and a political event. It tells the story of how a community comes to look together to see that justice is done. As such, it is one of the deepest meditations on human beings as moral and law abiding beings, and on what is necessary to restore individuals, families, and communities when they have been violated. But it is even more than a meditation on justice and punishment, and more than a guide for those who make institutional arrangements for handling such matters. The trilogy itself, staged for citizen-spectators, contributes, as the courts do, to making justice visible. No wonder Aeschylus wanted to tell this story in the theater.

This chapter follows the order of Aeschylus's plays and, in doing so, it demands, as they do, that its readers be patient about the outcome. As in the *Oresteia,* the full meaning of suggestions at the beginning will come to light only towards the end. The first two parts, on the first two plays of the trilogy, discuss kinship and revenge in communities where the primary institution is family. This discussion focuses on the theme of vision. Part 1, on *Agamemnon,* explores the inadequacies of private justice in communities where outsiders have almost no visual access into the affairs of private households, and have little power to act on what little they can see. Here private justice takes the form of revenge, in which satisfaction is closely related to the looking of the actors. An examination of Clytemnestra as the stage director of a symbolic drama that convicts her husband in her eyes suggests that, when justice later becomes public, it must still somehow exhibit the violator as she does. Part 2 shows that, in the *Libation Bearers,* Argos is still a city in which justice is executed from within the family. But the middle play opens a passageway between the restricted views and cyclic revenge of *Agamemnon* and the full view and conclusive justice promised in the *Eumenides.* Again, the discussion focuses on what is visible and on who is watching. Part 3, on the *Eumenides,* describes the genesis in Athens of fully visible public law in a community of citizens fully on view to each other. Publicly staged trials resembling theatrical dramas replace the privately staged dramas of Clytemnestra. They clearly articulate the alleged violation, and require the accused and the accuser to face each other in the sight of their shared community. Foreign relations, as well as judicial arrangements, develop as even outsiders become visible in the city. Under the aegis of Athena, Orestes is acquitted of his matricide and the age-old deities of blood revenge are assimilated into the civic order.

But even as it celebrates this humane and intelligent solution, the last play raises deep questions about political enlightenment and the effects of rational institutional judicial arrangements. Part 3 articulates what may be lost, as well as what is gained in the formation of a community of citizen-spectators. Looking at ourselves in the the light of the *Oresteia,* parts 3 and 4 ask what we can learn from Argos, as well as from Athens, as we constitute our own judicial and penal institutions. Finally, the discussion returns to Aeschylus's theater. Partly drama, partly trial, the tragedy itself supplements the political function of the courts by making its enlightened spectators look once more on the claims of Clytemnestra and the Furies. Together, Athena and Aeschylus might make it possible for Athenians to look together and see justice done.

Part One:
The House about the Hearth: Agamemnon

The *Agamemnon* repeatedly displays people whose fortunes are determined by a reigning family, but who are excluded from full action in the affairs of that family. Dependent upon their masters, attached to their *oikos* (house, household), most of them are primarily onlookers. They observe alone or together, but they do not constitute a full community of observers. They stand on the roof or before the gates, hoping for a message, imagining what is happening within. The Watchman, Chorus, and Cassandra are haunted by the violations of the House of Atreus, but cannot affect events. Their visions of the past are filled with accounts of others who witnessed and appealed with their eyes, but for whom there could never be full justice. Clytemnestra, unlike these outsiders, takes action in her own case. Twisted though she is, her deeds and the account she gives of herself must be taken seriously, even as more enlightened, civilized arrangements supersede her bloody personal revenge.

The trilogy begins with the solitary Watchman lying "dogwise" upon the roof of the palace, waiting for a signal light. Beyond the announcement expected of him, he is not free to speak: there's an "ox on his tongue" (36). Obedient watchdog to the house, he looks not only on his own behalf, but on orders from the queen. His ambiguous, riddling speech is disturbing, yet he cries for her to rise from her bed and raise an *ololugmos* (a joyous cry, 28) for the victorious return of her husband. He thinks not only of the queen, but of the whole household and of the gods. "Gods" (*theous*) is his first word and, thus, the first word of the play. He cannot see these gods. But he has been able to observe the distant processions of heavenly dynasties, and looks forward to the joyful earthly processions that will greet his lord's homecoming. But by the time he finishes speaking, it is clear that something is very wrong in Argos. He says he too will "make a choral prelude" (31), but we never see him dance, or even speak, with another. The anticipated "choirs of multitudes in Argos" (23) never materialize. As the Chorus enters, the Watchman remains fixed upon the roof, a permanently immobilized spectator. We never see him again.

The Chorus comes on in full motion, but the dancing of its members soon serves to emphasize how immobilized they also are. Unlike the Watchman, they look as a group, but their looking, too, is ineffectual. Ares, the war god, is no longer in these aged witnesses (78); they are "no stronger than a child" (81). Like the Watchman, they have no public role. Unlike other tragic choruses, they are never consulted or confided in by their rulers. Their authority is not political, but mantic; they have only "singing power" (106). Positioned always outside the gates of the great *oikos,* unable to see within, they turn their vision upon the past, depicting past events as if they could see them, making present in our eyes even pictures they never saw. By making memory visible, they gain some control over the past in which they may have muttered, but had no say. The Chorus speaks repeatedly of people who have no shame, who behave as if no one is watching. Like the Watchman, the Chorus looks to the gods, who are "not unregardful" (*ouk askopoi,* 461) of murderers. The Furies will strike down the unjust person and send him or her to "obscurity" (*amauron*) among the "unseen" (*aistois,* 463–67). On his return to Argos, Agamemnon explains how the gods cast votes for Ilium and all her people to be destroyed. His anachronistic image suggests the Athenian jurors we shall see in the third play, but the image is shattered by the thought of the "bloody urn" into which the gods cast their pebbles (815). Immortal voting does not bring an end to the cyclical vendettas of mortals. The mortals are agents of the gods, and the righting of one violation always brings a new one.

Aeschylus's Zeus, like the all-seeing gods in Homer, watches all, but he himself is not visible to mortals. Awesome power, he has no looks, no shape; he is never made manifest on stage. His justice is certain, but unpredictable, murky, a source of fear more than of confidence. His bird omen, for example, was "clear-seen" (*phanentes*) and "watched by all" (*pampreptois,* 116–17), but only the mantic seer could say what it meant. Calchas, standing slightly outside the human community, observes what the others observe, and is able to interpret the mysterious signs of the god. But Calchas's vision, like that of many mantics, gives no guidance for action. Although he is a trustworthy seer, he contributes little to the political foresight of the community whose eyes he is. Zeus is sure to strike down shameless violators who act as though he's not looking, but he is very remote from the people, the *oikos,* and the city that he oversees. And it soon becomes clear that there are many deities in the world, and that they often impose conflicting demands on the mortals who look to them for guidance. In *Agamemnon*, perplexed mortals speak repeatedly about their futures in the subjunctive or optative. Agamemnon, with one eye on the gods, sighs, "May all be well" (217), as he resolves to kill his daughter. Even for those who are not torn by conflicting demands, who respect Zeus and regard the right, there is no assurance of prosperity. All they can say is, "Sing sorrow, sorrow, but may good win out" (121).

As the Chorus describes it, Agamemnon surely was given a difficult choice at Aulis. But it is clear that, once he made his decision, he acted sacreligiously, as if no god or human would notice and judge. Aeschylus emphasizes the way it *looked*. Iphigeneia on the altar, "lovely as in a painted scene" (242), struck her murderers with "eyes' arrows of pity" (241). But neither her eyes, nor the appeals of witnesses, nor the consciousness of all-seeing gods, deterred her daring sacrificers. She looked in vain for justice. Like the Watchman and the Chorus, she was also limited in her motion and speech. Bound and gagged, her speech overcome by force, her only appeal to justice was her stifled "curse on the house" (237).

In a later ode, the Chorus remembers Helen. She, too, behaved as if no one was watching. They emphasize the ephemerality of her presence and her beauty. Aeschylus never makes her visible on stage. The audience "sees" only the effects she has had on others. Her own lack of responsibility is intensified because no one ever really responded to *her* crime. Despite the vast disruptions that result from the crimes of Paris and Helen, there is no disinterested *public* examination. The citizens and prophets of Argos were mere onlookers to the violation in the great house. A royal family was insulted. Obligated to save face, it pursued a great war in a private vendetta fought by unwilling citizens and ambitious foreigners. Paris and his city are punished; the Argives win the war. But Menelaus is a loser. How can the victory address his loss? After she left, Helen's "traces" (*stiboi*) remain in his bed, and a "phantom" (*phasma*) seems to rule the house. But in the "blank gaze of his eyes, all Aphrodite is gone"; the "vision" (*opsis*) slips from his hands (414–26). After the war, the Herald reports that Menelaus, like Helen, is now "lost to sight" (*aphantos*, 624). For the violations that reduced her husband and many young Argives to nothing, Helen is never visibly punished. There is not even a private face-to-face reckoning. As a result, the case is never really brought to a conclusion. Menalaus's visions are of Helen before she betrayed him. He does not imagine her in the act of violation. The legends tell how, after the war, he restored her to their "home." But his manhood is never restored. Homer completes the story of Helen and Menelaus in book 4 of the *Odyssey*, one of the most painful and poignant depictions ever written of looking the other way.[1] Helen, whom the gods have made barren, offers a memory-deadening drug to allow herself and her husband to keep up appearances. Despite their decorum, we, and all who know their story, find it hard to look.

Let us return now to the living protagonists of the *Agamemnon*, to their views of justice, and to further connections between viewing and justice. Clytemnestra, like Menelaus, has been filled with visions: beacon signs from Troy, her daughter's murder, the children of Thyestes and Troy, dreams of her husband's gashed body at Troy, and that body seen in the flesh. In her private thoughts and in her dreams, she has rehearsed her injuries and staged her revenge. She depicts herself as a "watchdog of the house" (607). To see justice done, she must take justice into her own hands. She anticipates Agamemnon's reentry into the house:

> what light
> is sweeter than this for woman to behold, to
> spread the gates before her husband home from
> war and saved by a god? (602)

This opening of the "gates" (*pylas*) to her husband is the first of many such openings in the trilogy, some of which will reveal things too horrible to look upon. As we shall see in part 2, moving through the gates will become a major theme. But for now, her sense of justice requires that, not only the distant gods, but she herself and other human observers witness the wrongs Agamemnon has committed. Unlike Menelaus, she requires a showdown. What exactly does she need to see?

Clytemnestra persuades him to walk on tapestries. These cloths are woven, embroidered, and dipped in precious dyes. Trampling them means destroying the visible work of the *oikos*, its labor and cooperation, its accumulated wealth, which should not be taken for granted, even when it is plentiful. The woven tapestries hold the *oikos* together. Birth-clothes, bedclothes, and death-clothes are the visible signs of the coherence of a family in time.[2] The violations of others in this story are often associated with the disregard of household goods: Paris "trampled on the delicacy of things inviolable" (371–72), and Helen walked lightly away from the soft curtains of her marriage bed. When

Agamemnon sacrificed Iphigeneia, her dyed saphron robes fell "to the ground" (239). Now, before the house, Clytemnestra forces him to imitate his disregard for the blood of his family in his disregard for the blood-red possessions of their house. Once inside, he will be bound by the very bonds he chose to break. Even his temporary reluctance here recapitulates his hesitation at Aulis. She has proven him guilty.

There is another way in which the welcome scene displays his violations. By making him walk on tapestries, she keeps him from touching the ground he has come home to. His separation from the ground, like his trampling of precious goods, recapitulates the ways he has already violated the earth. The House of Atreus pours blood on the ground: the blood of Thyestes' children and Iphigeneia, of the innocent Trojan young, and of all the young Argives who died for the Atreids' quarrel and were buried in the wrong ground (452–55). Agamemnon destroyed Troy and the ground it stood on. There is a special horror about this. The way in which he returns home reflects his violations of home ground. Compare him with the earthy Herald who repeatedly greets the land, the earth in which he now knows he'll be buried (503–7). In the *Odyssey*, Odysseus kisses dry land after emerging from the sea (V.463); when he learns he has set foot on his own home, he rejoices in the land and "he kissed it" (XIII.354). Homer's Agamemnon, whose sacrifice of Iphigeneia is never mentioned, is an innocent who comes home to be murdered by the evil Aegisthus. Like Odysseus, he "clasped his native land and kissed it" (IV.522). When Aeschylus's Agamemnon returns home, his deliberate separation from family and *oikos* is represented by his separation from his own earth. He does not kiss the earth, and Clytemnestra does not let him touch it. Not until the second play, in the family burial ground, will he resume his proper relation to the *oikos* and its earth.

Why must Clytemnestra *see* Agamemnon in this way before she murders him in revenge? The "carpet scene," with its tense arguments and vivid red props, is always said to be the most dramatic in the play. It is, indeed, a staged representation for herself and, in some tentative way, for her spectators in Argos. The theatrical *agôn* that she produces is a test, a trial, not in the full sense the word comes to have by the end of the trilogy, but like it in that it questions and exhibits the man whom she must judge. It re-views symbolically the acts of which he is accused: destroying the household goods and children, and violating the earth. She has, of course, convicted and killed him several times already, imagining his violations in her dreams and in her thoughts. Now, at last, she welcomes him, not to restore him to their unravelled home, but to provide herself with the incriminating evidence she needs to convict him. Justice (*dikê*) entails showing (*deiknumi*)[3] the accused for what he is. After seeing and exhibiting his violations, she herself is prepared to execute justice.

Agamemnon, the chief character in her drama, is deeply disturbed by the confrontation, and is self-conscious about the various spectators—the people and the gods—who watch the conqueror trample his household goods. Although he must be aware that he is on trial for his life and that the carpet scene displays his guilt, he never *acknowledges* that the incident tries and convicts him. To do so would be politically impossible. The charges are not articulated and evidence is not discussed. His defense also must be in code: vague disclaimers about trampling purple tapestries, and whether Priam would do it. He cries out from the bath, from "within" (*eso*, 1343) the house to no one in particular, and dies without publicly defending his innocence or acknowledging his guilt. The presence of a third person, Cassandra, who witnesses the murder and then is executed as further "evidence" in his case, makes the privacy of the case even more striking, especially since she is literally a seer.

Cassandra at first looks like one of those Aeschylean extras included to be seen but not heard. Though she becomes the primary speaker for three hundred lines at the moment of greatest suspense in the play, she retains something of this first visual character. She herself is a true visionary whose verbal power lies not in reasoned argument, but in picture painting. She comes from a distant kingdom with eyewitness reports of its destruction. But she also sees through the gates of the house to which she's been brought, and knows what is about to happen and why. Crying "look, look" (*idou, idou*, 1125) and "see" (*horate*, 1217), she depicts the ancient and present horrors of the family that dwells within.

But the Chorus wants no prophets. Usually disturbed by their inability to see very much, these feeble elders now would rather look away. Cassandra insists that the Chorus bear her witness (1317) as she bore witness to the earlier horrors she now depicts. As a mere "martyr"—the Greek means "witness"—she, like the Watchman and the Chorus, has little to contribute to the effecting of justice. It is her special curse to have no one understand or believe what she says. Seemingly incoherent, "her eye turned inward," she speaks in a different meter from the Chorus.[4] Her dance is solitary, frantic, erratic. She dances up to the gates and is repeatedly repelled, entering only to die, the last evidence of Agamemnon's guilt, the last revealing element in the tableau Clytemnestra has arranged in the bath. Before Cassandra enters, she speaks of her imminent death, identifying the palace gates with the gates of Hades, and prays:

> that the stroke be true,
> and that with no convulsion, with a rush of blood
> in painless death, I may close up these eyes, and rest. (1291–94).

In her last speech, no longer mantic and wild, she asks that the avengers who strike her murderers avenge as well "one simple slave who died, a small thing, lightly killed" (1325–26). Earlier she said that Agamemnon and she must die, but not "vengeless by the gods" (1279), for another avenger will return, a "mother-killing scion, and avenger of his father" (1280–81). Although Cassandra includes herself in this anticipated revenge, justice is never done with respect to her. True to her prophecy, Orestes eventually returns as avenger, but only for his father. So far as we know, Cassandra is never mentioned again—by the Chorus, Orestes, gods, or human court. Her own family, annihilated by her new master, has already entered Hades, and, in her world, revenge and mourning rites are the responsibility of kin; she will have neither. Among the *oikoi* of Argos, there is no justice for a stateless foreigner. The only character with no social significance,[5] she can only claim a "stranger's grace" (*epixenoumai*, 1320). Cassandra dies a witness, not only to the deaths of Thyestes' children, Agamemnon, and the people of Troy, but also to the inadequacies of divine justice in the case of a human girl once touched by a god who turned against her. The Chorus first begged Clytemnestra to "be healer" (*paiôn*, 98). But Cassandra, made sick by a god called "healer" (146, 512), knows that "no healer stands over this story" (1248). She vividly paints her pictures, but like her they are ephemeral, preserved in the stories of poets and priests, but providing no binding precedents in the affairs of mortals. Like the Watchman, the Chorus, and Iphigeneia, her body is bound, her speech is impaired. She can only watch, curse, and hope that things will come right in the end.

> Alas, poor men, their destiny. When all goes well a shadow will overthrow it. If it be unkind one stroke of a wet sponge wipes all the picture out; and that is far the most unhappy thing of all. (1327–30)

After Cassandra enters the palace, we see the twelve[6] Argive elders—it is likely that the Chorus members speak serially—again excluded from the action, unable to see the crime they know is being committed. Not part of the family or household, their position is fixed outside the gates that restrict their vision. They cannot enter to act at the private hearth, though they know that their future, too, will be determined by what takes place within. Those insiders who "trample to the ground deliberation's honor" (1356–57) may soon subject these connected outsiders to tyranny. "It is clear to see" (*horan paresti*, 1354), yet there are no eyewitnesses, so how can they be certain about what has happened? The king, as we have seen, cries out from within to no one in particular. Even the brief deliberation of the Chorus is fragmented. The Chorus members wish to "take counsel together" (1347), but the twelve voices do not speak to each other; the action upon which they agree is to take no action. They are paralyzed because they have no recognized access to what has occurred within; "to guess" (*topazein*) is not "to know clearly" (*saph'eidenai*, 1369). A frantic, erratic dance should accompany this fragmented consultation. We have yet to see true communal speech or motion in the *Oresteia*. This will come only when a community can arrange to look together.

Violent deeds in most Greek tragedies are reported by eyewitness messengers who make us see what cannot be shown on stage. The deaths of Antigone, Jocasta, and Pentheus, for example, are narrated by outsiders whose personal importance to the action is negligible. But in *Agamemnon*, Clytemnestra—the play's protagonist, the murderer herself—once more appears at the palace gates, attempting to communicate with those who are defined by being outside them. She is shameless as she describes the obscene carnage and exhibits her own bloodied hands. Before we dismiss her as primitive or merely aberrant in her desire for personal revenge, we must try to understand how she understands herself and why she exhibits what she has done.

Just as before she punishes him, she must see for herself his violations—or, at least, reenactments of them—so she herself must strike him down and see his reaction. The offstage murder and her description emphasize that there are *two* blows, followed by a third. Surely, in the brief moment between those first two blows, the eyes of the "defendant" meet those of his "victim," "accuser," and "judge," to satisfy her, one last time, that she is indeed executing justice. Between the two blows, Agamemnon must acknowledge, albeit silently, that he is being punished.[7] And she must *feel* his death and *see* it with her own eyes; the Chorus says she has blood in them. To satisfy her, his punishment must be literally firsthand: "This is Agamemnon, my husband, a corpse, the work of this right hand, a righteous craftsman'' (1404–6). She has already described his death:

Thus falling he gasps out his life, pouring forth a sharp spurt of blood and hits me with a dark sprinkling of bloody dew—I rejoicing not less than the sown corn bursting the bud rejoices in the god-given rain. (1388–92)

This horrifying passage, and the whole preceding report, are in the present tense. Once again, she is an eyewitness recreating the scene for herself and for the audience. Why does she represent her satisfaction in this extraordinary image of ritual sacrifice, moist fecundity, and birth?

It is because Agamemnon's violations had, in some way, killed his wife. Her almost superhuman energy in the earlier part of the play has a dry brittleness about it; it is associated with fires and great distances. It is a paralyzed, pent-up energy of strained waiting and watching. Agamemnon has been gone ten years, has killed the ''dearest labor'' (1417) of her womb, the ''young shoot'' of their love (1525), and replaced his wife with ''every Chryseis at Troy'' (1439). She, in turn, has contaminated her womb by taking in an inferior man, an enemy of her husband's house. The adultery destroys Agamemnon as her husband before she destroys his life. Though she has taken up with Aegisthus, and intends to continue this union, Clytemnestra's murder of Agamemnon has little to do with lust for his successor. Nor, as some suggest, does it express her resentment at being denied sexual gratification by Agamemnon's long absence.

Rather, the murder and her staging and restaging of it are about another kind of lust—the lust for revenge—which, denied satisfaction, burns out the survivor, making continued life impossible for her as well as for her dead kin. Only the death of Iphigeneia's murderer can refertilize her mother's womb. In a way, Aegisthus is irrelevant. Killing Agamemnon cannot bring Iphigeneia back from the dead, but it does seem to restore her mother to life.[8] She anticipates this rebirth before he returns. Her first words in the play are images of wombs and birth, of ''reborn'' light, and she greets her returning husband in elaborate strained metaphors of refreshment and rebirth: he is the ''running spring a parched wayfarer strays upon'' (901), and ''When the root lives, yet the leaves will come again'' (966). Later, describing her revenge, she almost dances with satisfaction.

The imagery of thirst and hunger in connection with revenge is a commonplace. To satisfy, justice must be seen and even ''tasted.''

Hamlet's cry, "Now could I drink hot blood," is the cry of all avengers. He, too, arranges to represent—in a real play—the guilt of the wrongdoer. "The Mousetrap" moves the would-be avenger as much as it "catches" the "conscience of the king" (III.ii). It is his most vigorous attempt to respond to his father's ghost's exhortation, "Remember me." In the *Iliad*, Zeus tells Hera:

> If you were to enter the gates and great walls and eat Priam raw and Priam's children and the other Trojans, then you might heal your anger. (IV.34–36)

Books later, the mortal Achilles, refusing to eat with his comrades, says that ransom, and even death, would not satisfy his hunger for revenge against Hector:

> Would that in any wise wrath and fury might bid me carve your flesh and eat it raw, because of what you have wrought. (XXII.346–47)

Would-be avengers also imagine feeding the corpses of their enemies to dogs and birds. In the revealing old legends, they actually do eat their enemies.[9] The Chorus imagines Clytemnestra standing above the corpse of her husband, like a carrion crow (1472–73). She identifies herself with the old "avenger" (Thyestes) of the House of Atreus. The voluptuous satisfaction of her hunger for revenge is retaliation in kind for all their crimes, finally summed up in the horrifying descriptions of the "feast" of Thyestes, in which he made his victim eat an abominable meal—his own children. Like the Fury with whom she also identifies, she is eaten away by the memories of past wrongs. Unlike the diminished Menelaus, who lives on with barren Helen, drugging himself to forget the painful past, Clytemnestra, true to her name ("famed memory," *klutos, mnêmê*), restores herself by remembering and retaliating. Revenge is sweet as she sprinkles herself with the blood of the man who wronged her.

The showers of blood, water, and rain that revitalize Clytemnestra soon turn into her own horror, for, by murdering, she contaminates herself and must herself be punished. By the end of *Agamemnon*, the house is falling, the rain turns bloody (1533), the harvest monstrous, and the reaping time bitter (1655). In the *Libation Bearers*, all her libations turn to blood and tears, her milk to blood. But, though it is temporary, the intense sweetness of her revenge suggests that the very violence of the passion behind her act may be connected with the fruitfulness and flowering of human things. It is somehow appropriate to human nature to want to take justice into one's own hands, and to bloody those hands in doing so. Her argument with the Chorus suggests the law court and trial in the third play, but without the "legal framework" and the "independent arbitrator" at work there.[10] This scene clearly points to the later one in that it offers a challenge to the city law that will replace the blood revenge depicted here: how can an antiseptic civil justice of clean hands and no more blood on the ground satisfy the survivors as well as the reviving rain of blood in the first play seems to do? Such blood rituals are clearly incompatible with civilized life. As we have seen, before Clytemnestra bloodies her hands, she must *see* Agamemnon reenact his crimes. By executing him herself, she also literally sees to it that he is punished. Perhaps enlightened institutional justice can remember her needs by attending to the importance of *seeing* for those who have been wounded. Finally, perhaps these wounded can be made fully whole again only when a whole city comes to *see* in a way not possible in Argos.

Agamemnon deteriorates at the end into unresolved bickering between the Chorus and Aegisthus, who first appears late in the play. Unlike Homer's Aegisthus, Aeschylus's Aegisthus does not do the killing. He claims to have been in on the planning, but Clytemnestra mentions him only as her protector.[11] Although Aegisthus, too, speaks of revenge, the fact that he does not bloody his own hands makes him seem less serious than Clytemnestra. To the Chorus's feeble curses and vague hopes for Orestes' return, Aegisthus opposes threats of violence. Clytemnestra now speaks "as a woman" for reconciliation, urging all to return to their homes (*pros domous*, 1657), and assuring Aegisthus that he and she have the power to bring good order to their house (*dômatôn*, 1673). As they enter the palace, the elders retreat, leaving the theater spectators with a last view of the closed gates and the now empty roof. What has become of the Watchman and his hopes for a great public celebration? The actors go off separately or in fragmented groups; *Agamemnon* does not end with an exit procession.[12] Argos is not yet a fully constituted community.

The last word of *Agamemnon*, "house" (*dômatôn*),[13] reminds us that the primary experience for the human beings in this play is still family. Repeatedly, the *oikos* is defined as the "house [*oikos, domos*] about the hearth" (427, 851, 968). Its men depart to fight a distant enemy, also spoken of as a father and his people (537, 747). The victorious Achaians send messages back over vast distances across unpeopled cliffs and streams, rocks and mountains, between places connected, not by roads, but by beacon fires. There are guest-friends (*xenoi*) as well as enemies out there—Odysseus and Strophius are mentioned—but developed international relations are not part of this world. Though they roam far from home, for these men, as well as for their women, *place* is determined by the hearth. The Chorus says that Clytemnestra offers sacrifices to the gods of the city, to those above and those below, and to the gods of the sky and marketplace (88–90), but she mentions the gods only as they relate to her family. The Herald is overjoyed to return to his native land, but he speaks only briefly of the "gods of the marketplace" (513). The rest of the play gives us little sense of public places in Argos, either of natural places or of those built by humans—of roads, common altars, or buildings—other than the great palace whose facade dominates the stage. When Agamemnon returns from Troy, he speaks of the business of the "city and the gods," and says he'll convene a full council of citizens (844–46). But his attention is on his own hall, the "house about the hearth" (*domous ephestios*, 851). He does not go to a temple to make offerings to the common gods, but to the fire in his own house.[14] "The focus is the *focus*."[15] First and foremost a household patriarch, this monarch has no obligation to share his deliberations with council or jurors. They may look, but only at his discretion.

The status of any place between nature's place—mountains, soil, and earth—and the hearth-place is vague. Between *theous* in the first line and *dômatôn* at the end, there is an immense gap. Between the great gods and the family hearth, there is little to look to or at. Distant gods and next of kin watch and act to insure a kind of justice in the world of mortals. But what takes place at the hearth is secret, concealed from the view of mortal strangers.[16]

Deep in the past, a brother stole his brother's wife. As punishment he was forced unknowingly to eat—to reabsorb—his own children. This grotesque story is the horrifying image of the turning inward that is characteristic of Argos. Until these mortals move beyond the family, their justice can be, at best, only temporarily satisfying. There must be a more effective passage between inside and outside, between the hearth and the city, between the city and other cities, a passage that would allow for a better view.

Part Two:
Through the Gates: The Libation Bearers

In the *Libation Bearers*, Aeschylus rehabilitates the *oikos* violator, Agamemnon, now dead and no longer visible to his kin. The restoration occurs in the first part of the play, as the surviving kin become once more visible to each other. This happens with the help of observers who are part of the household, although they are not blood relations. Unlike the observers in the first play, their presence is recognized by the family, and they consult freely in the course of the action. The Chorus in the first part of the play, and Pylades later, urges action and is heeded. The drama that bridges kin revenge in Argos and the court trial in Athens widens the vision of all the actors, both insiders and outsiders. Though there is not yet a full city of assembled onlookers, the *Libation Bearers* depicts a significant shift in view.

In *Agamemnon*, most of the king's next-of-kin are out of sight. Iphigeneia is dead, and the young Orestes has been sent to a guest-friend in Phocis to avoid his witnessing the murder or becoming the visible focus of resistance to Aegisthus and Clytemnestra. In the early stages of the story, Electra is never mentioned; no one even catches a glimpse of her. The *Libation Bearers* opens with the long-absent Orestes trying to make sense of what he sees in the family burial ground. The female Chorus enters furtively, perhaps separately, carrying libations, speaking of its terror and forebodings. At this point, the Chorus might remind us of the Watchman and Chorus of the *Agamemnon*. Too much blood has stained this ground and the house is hidden in darkness. Electra, too, fears to look or to be seen:

> quiet and dishonored, as my father died
> shall I pour out this offering for the ground to drink,
> and go, like one who empties garbage out of doors,
> and turn my eyes, and throw the vessel far away. (96–99)

Before she and her surviving kin can come together to act, they must properly recognize each other. The *Libation Bearers*, like *Agamemnon*, opens with the interpretation of visual symbols. The flares from distant Troy are "proofs" (*tekmêria*) (*Ag.*, 352) across vast unknown places. But the signs interpreted in the Atreid burial ground are local and personal. They are necessary to restore the violated *oikos* and its members. "On trial" for the first time, Orestes shows himself for what he is. Unlike his father in the previous play, he exhibits, not his separation from the *oikos*, but his attachment to it. As he presents proofs of his identity, he exhorts Electra to look at the exhibits, to recognize visually—the passage (225 ff.) contains a string of vision words—something she remembers from another time. As the

Chorus has told her, just before she sees the offerings, memory is essential to family justice. The hair is recognizable because it looks like her own (174–76); it could belong to no other of the townspeople (188). There is a second piece of "evidence" (*tekmêrion*, 205): one of the sets of footsteps resembles hers. Again, her natural love and liking belong to what is visibly like her. At first, Electra and the Chorus think Orestes has sent the hair offering because, as an exile, "He can never again set foot upon this land" (182); they think he is dead to them. But he has returned, and his footprints, recognized, like his hair, by their *looks*, are signs of the first proper "stepping" in the *Oresteia*. Orestes' homecoming, unlike his father's, is characterized by tears and the careful placing of his foot on home ground. Unlike the kicking, trampling missteps of the *Agamemnon*, these steps are the first steps toward reconstituting this household in the eyes of its dead and living members and in the eyes of the gods. But, as we shall see, the middle play makes it clear that the reconstitution of the household will also require "middle" witnesses—visible and identifiable observers between those who are personally involved and the far-seeing but too-distant gods.

Having offered her visual evidence in the hair and tracks, Orestes exhorts Electra to "look" (*idou,* 231) at a last proof that he is her brother. The small piece of weaving, a bit of swaddling clothes, or baby blanket, identifies him as native to this *oikos*. Like his nurse's memories later in the play, they remind us of a time before the fabric of this family was torn apart. Helen's abandoned bedclothes, Iphigeneia's dropped mantle, Clytemnestra's trampled tapestries, and the woven nets in which she killed her man, all recede when Electra examines a scrap of cloth, and recognizes the "dearest treasured darling of my father's house," a "joyful sight" (*terpnon omma*) who brings back "four lives to me" (235–38). By recognizing each other in the family burial ground, these children of the house, one an exile and the other like an outcast slave, can, for the first time, feel that they are at home.

As we have seen, the gods witness all that mortals do. Spectators on high, they judge and punish but are not themselves very much affected by what they see. Beneath the earth, there is another assembly of spectators, ancestral watchers who are also deities in some way. The earth they dwell in is local ground, attached to a particular house and family that live on it. Like that of the gods, "The wrath of the [dead] father" also "comes unseen" (*oukh horômenên,* 293–94). But as members of the *oikos* extended through time, living on somehow beneath the earth, the deified dead relatives, unlike the detached immortal Olympians, are influenced by what the living do. Libations poured on their graves keep them alive to the living, just as flowers and green plants in our cemeteries keep our dead somehow alive to us. The children sense that their ancestor watches over them and expects—looks forward to—their action: "Earth, let my father emerge to watch me fight" (*epopteusai makhên*, 489).

Two things are expected of Agamemnon's surviving kin. Since he was denied proper burial and mourning rites (*Ag.*, 1554; *L.B.*, 439–44, 982), they must see to it that these ritual ceremonies are completed. For them to go on living, it is necessary for him to be laid to rest. Second, they must retaliate for his violent death. Like Clytemnestra, until they *see* his murderers punished, they remain unsatisfied, just as they would be if the funeral rites were not completed.

Electra and Orestes come into focus to each other in the presence of living witnesses, as well as dead ancestral onlookers. Unlike the male Chorus in *Agamemnon*, the female Chorus of the *Libation Bearers* is part of the Atreid *oikos*. Privy to the internal affairs of this family, the Chorus may even enter the orchestra from inside the palace gates.[17] Unlike the excluded Argive elders, this Chorus watches from *within*. They share the hearth and pour libations in the burial ground. It is important that they are outsiders who have been absorbed into the household. Electra invites them as friends to share in counsel, for they now share a "common enemy in the house" (*koinon . . . ekhthos en domois*, 101). Taken from their own fathers' houses (76–77), now friendly others to part of this adopted new house, these slave women from foreign lands—perhaps from Troy—urge action on behalf of a murdered father. In the early scene, they are oppressed by fear. But once their young masters are reunited, they express their views clearly, are consulted, and even, at one point, tell their superiors when to stop speaking (265). Orestes tells them "to be silent" or "speak in the way that will help us" (582), and they are responsible for Aegisthus's return without bodyguards (770–73). These inside-outside witnesses affirm the principle of the first play, that justice must come from the blood relatives of those who have been injured:

> Here in the house there lies the cure for this, not to be brought from outside, never from others but in themselves. (471–74)

When the time for action comes, these women are out of view, and they do not see those who act. They hear Aegisthus's cry and ask,

"What has been done in the house?" (871). But, unlike the confused and excluded Chorus of *Agamemnon*, this Chorus knows what is happening inside. Likewise, when Orestes is killing Clytemnestra, it knows exactly what he is doing and why. The Chorus members speak clearly and in concert, dancing together. Orestes reappears after only forty lines, as if to report that he has fulfilled their expectations. Although their relief is soon seen to be illusory, the "witnesses" of this "just revenge" are clearly different from Cassandra and the impotent Argive elders.

Another observer accompanies Orestes in his homecoming and revenge. Like Cassandra, Pylades stands silently on stage through most of the play. But, unlike Cassandra's long mantic speech and ineffectual visions, Pylades' one brief line and his presence as a discerning observer are crucial to the story of the Atreids. They, too, signal a move from the dark confines of house and kin to the clearer light of streets and cities. Ever since Agamemnon yielded to persuasion in the form of a woman and entered the palace gates, there has been no masculine presence on stage; we have been occupied with the powerless Argive Chorus, the effeminate Aegisthus, and with Electra, Clytemnestra, Cilissa, and the Chorus of slave women. The return of two vigorous young men to Argos signals a shift to the world of men, always less attached to the *oikos,* and, even more important, a shift to a tie beyond the *oikos.* Though Orestes has returned as the son of the House of Atreus, his long but not permanent, exile, no doubt, has widened his point of view.[18] With Pylades, Orestes can be both insider and outsider.

Pylades is the son of Strophius of Phocis, the guest-friend to whom Clytemnestra exiled Orestes. He is from outside the Atreid family; the footprints he leaves in the burial ground are clearly different (208). He has accompanied Orestes as a friend whose ties are by choice, not by nature. He comes as another self who is truly other. From his first appearance, the presence of this stranger is jarring; outsiders are usually excluded from the family burial ground.[19] For nine hundred lines, he stands silent in this private place, but he is fully visible. At the crucial moment, he urges distance from internal ties. He speaks in the name of a sworn oath and the oracle of Apollo at Pytho, a cosmopolitan, not local or family, shrine. Pylades' brief speech is clear. It is a question that requires thought and an answer. His persuasion is not the murky and feminine Peitho that moved Agamemnon at Aulis or before the palace, but a rational reminder of the way in which words hold a man to sworn promises. We are beginning to move from the ambiguous language of songs, supplications, wishes, and curses to a more public discourse. And Pylades stands still. Though he too speaks for kin revenge, unlike the Chorus, he is no dancer. Pylades reminds Orestes of the absolute justice of family revenge, but the verbal exchange points toward political and judicial speech in the third play. The legal language in which Orestes responds to Pylades also points to the impending trial.

Aeschylus plays on the name of Pylades as he plays earlier with the names of Zeus (*Ag.*, 160-66), Helen (*Ag.*, 688-89), Apollo (*Ag.*, 1080–82), and Pallas Athena (*Eum.*, 753–54).[20] When Electra and the women are sent into the house, the men remain outside. Orestes, who earlier proved himself an insider by his looks and words, now temporarily distances himself. Disguised as an outlander with a foreign accent, he will "go to the outer gates with Pylades" (*eph' herkeious pylas Pyladei,* 561–62). The following lines (565–71) emphasize the anticipated crossing of the threshold. The next time we see Orestes and Pylades, they are knocking at the "gates" (*pylai*) and are admitted by Clytemnestra. Shortly after, they finally penetrate the innermost gates of the house in which Orestes will kill his mother.

In *Agamemnon*, the feeble Chorus stands outside the palace gates with no sure knowledge or part to play as murderous justice takes place within. Cassandra witnesses these murders before they occur, but she speaks only of the gates of Hades (*Ag.*, 1291). In *Agamemnon*, Clytemnestra keeps appearing at the gates to justify what she's done within, but no true communication with those outside is possible. In the *Libation Bearers*, the Chorus stands outside the house, but it has been within and it is instrumental in preparing for the action that occurs within. Pylades, first referred to as a "fellow wayfarer" (*sunemporou,* 208), is an outside witness who enters within the gates, and finally accompanies Orestes within the house. The justice he witnesses is the ancient justice of kin revenge, but his overseeing of the act previews the way in which an entire city of outsiders will some day penetrate the walls of private households. They will see that justice is done without requiring another relative's bloodied hands. The *Libation Bearers,* positioned between the *oikos* of *Agamemnon* and the city of the *Eumenides,* is the threshold we cross as we move toward making justice visible.[21]

As we have seen, Agamemnon goes to his death without explicitly acknowledging that he is being tried and punished. In the *Libation Bearers* also, the victim is trapped; this case, too, is closed from the beginning. But there is an important difference. As Clytemnestra faces her death, she acknowledges what is happening and explicitly makes a case for herself. The accusation is clear, and she and her accuser argue over the facts and motives. Thus, although this is still summary and private justice, it differs radically from her own symbolic exhibition of her victim's guilt and her retaliation, and from those of Thyestes and Atreus as well. The articulated confrontation with the accused is the first step into the light from dark revenge and feud justice to public trial. The accused, with her eyes wide open, is now a self-conscious observer, as well as participant, in her own trial and punishment.

As Orestes and Pylades take Clytemnestra to her death within the palace, the women outside express their sorrow for her, but reiterate their support for Orestes. The deed must be done "so that the eye of the house [*ophthalmon oikôn*] shall not utterly die" (934). They have looked to him, the most precious part of the family, as the leader who'll guide and look out for them. Now, naively, they look forward to the "end" of "this chain of bloodlettings" (933) to the "light that is here to behold [*idein*]" (961).

Orestes, who is as concerned to justify his deed as his mother was to justify hers, steps from within the palace and exhorts the spectators to "behold" (*idesthe*, 973) and "behold again" (*idesthe d'aute*, 980). Not only his own father, but father Helios, "the one overseeing all things" (*ho pant' epopteuon*, 985), may be his "witness" (*martys*) in his day of "justice" (*dikêi*) that he "justly" (*endikôs*) killed his mother (987–988):

> Did she do it or did she not? My witness (*martyrei*) is this great robe. It was thus she stained Aegisthus's sword. Dip it and dip it again, the smear of blood conspires with time to spoil the beauty of this precious thing. (1010–13)

By reenacting and rehearsing her crime in his own eyes and in those of the people he addresses, he displays her with her murder instrument and with her accomplice, and finds her guilty. Once again, to bring to justice (*dikê*) means to show (*deiknumi*), to re-present the acts of which the guilty is accused. After striking her down, he feels that he has completed the return to life that began in the cemetery at the play's opening.

But Orestes knows, almost immediately, that he cannot stay at home and resume an ordinary life after avenging his father's death. Unlike Clytemnestra, he knows that the retributions he insists on cannot revivify him or release him from the recurring Atreid curse. The inversions of Argos, previously expressed in Thyestes' eating his own children, are here represented in Clytemnestra's dream of the nursing snake that devours its own mother. Orestes' satisfaction is short-lived. In part, this is because, although he claims that "all men of Argos in time to come" will "witness" (*martyrein*) the evils he has righted (1040–41), at this time, Argos is not yet properly constituted as a *city* of witnesses. Pylades is a foreigner, ineffectual against family Furies, and he departs without speaking again. The Chorus is still female, foreign, house servants. Though they have suggested the outside, they are not yet an effective *city*. Unlike the old men at the end of *Agamemnon*, they have the last word. But they are still only stand-by witnessess, and the second play ends with a question. Here, too, there cannot yet be a proper exit procession. The Chorus should not be increased to a crowd for operatic stage effects at the end of the play.[22] The Chorus can see the evidence Orestes shows it but, like Pylades, it cannot see the hideous Furies who appear to him as the immediate consequence of his deed. Nor does Aeschylus allow the spectators in the theater to see them yet either. On these dread "bloodhounds of his mother's hate" (1054), he must look alone. Justice is still in the hands of private "watchdogs." Like Clytemnestra, they have blood in their eyes (1058). Their looks and the looking that supersedes their looking are the subjects of the third part of the trilogy.

Part Three:
From Furies to Juries: The Eumenides

The *Eumenides* identifies the founding of a public court with the foundation of the city. To avoid repeatedly bloodying the hands of the next just avenger, the community arranges to look together with those who have been personally wronged, and to see to it that the alleged violator will be impersonally acquitted or punished. As mortals begin to look for justice, not only to the gods and to their own kin, but to themselves as part of a wider community of mortals, the polis becomes a visible locus of action, peopled by public agents as well as private ones. Gods, city, citizens, and outsiders all look very different by the end of the trilogy.

We first see the Furies through the eyes of the Pythian priestess. She runs from the temple in horror at "things terrible to speak and terrible for the eyes to see" (*deina lexai, deina d'ophthalmois drakein*, 34). Apollo soon declares of the Furies that the "whole way of their shape

is guide" (*pas d'uphegeitai tropos morphês*, 192–93) to what they are.
Before this, the Furies have been seen only by those they pursue: by
Clytemnestra, as snakes in her guilty dream visions, and by Orestes
after he murders her. The first major step in the *Eumenides* is the one
the Furies take when they emerge from the temple and cross the
threshold into open daylight. At Delphi and at Athens, Aeschylus
makes them visible to all the stage characters, and, for the first time,
to the spectators in his audience. Let us look upon their shape and
what it reveals.

The looks of these Furies are the key to how they look at things.
Daughters of the Earth and Night, they are nether-divinities, wingless,
serpentine, essentially attached to place. Their peculiar place is dark
Tartarus below the earth. In their ministerings to mortals, they are
guardians of human beings as beings defined by the hearth-place.
Especially concerned with violations against parents, old age, and
suppliants, they preserve the sanctity of kin and blood relations,
relations among those who live, cook, and worship around the same
hearth. They also guard the arrangements humans have made for
providing for non-blood neighbors and guest-friends from distant
places, but always as they relate to the *oikos*. Low to the ground, they
care for the ground—as foundation, private altar, and burial place for
the *oikos*. No matter how far a violator flees from the place he has
violated, the Furies pursue him and keep him in place. Their song is a
"binding song"; their victim is forever bound to his origins.

Although the Furies are vigilantes, their pursuit is more visceral
than visual. They work in the dark, away from Helios, the sun god
(386, 396). Their eyes are gummy, ever sleepy, not the locus of their
primary sense. Like bloodhounds with noses to the ground, they smell
their evidence. It is not the *looks* of Orestes' footprints that attract
their attention. They grind their victims into the ground onto which
they drip poison (780–87). Like Clytemnestra, they are hungry for
revenge; they feed on their victims (304–5). They are "rememberers"
(*mnêmones*, 383), "witnesses" (*martyres*, 318), who bring infertility
and cancer on the seeing and the blind (322). But although they have a
long memory, they are shortsighted.[23] They strike indiscriminately,
often failing to distinguish an offender from those connected to him.
Thus, each act of justice is simultaneously a new violation. Furies
punish descendants for the sins of their ancestors, and strike down a
whole people for the crime of their prince. According to Furies-justice,
Thyestes' children, the sons of Atreus, and the children of Troy must
pay the price of their attachments.

Attached not only to place, the Furies are also attached to each other. Though later tradition represents them as three named individuals, here they are characterized as a "company" or "troop" (*lokhos*, 46), bearing only a collective name. The Priestess has difficulty describing their looks. They seem to be women—or partial women. Although in shape they resemble Gorgons or, perhaps, Harpies, they are not either; the essence of their shape is shapelessness. She first sees them as a single mass of intertwined, snaky bodies. They describe themselves as "linked" to each other (307). One production emphasized their attachment by bagging them into a physical heap.[24]

Like all choruses, this one must dance. But, unlike the old men or the slave women in the first two plays, the Furies are characteristically dancers. As guardians of place, these closely linked dancers who always retain their own close physical relation to the ground, aim to bring their victims down. One look at them reduces even the erect priestess of Apollo to all fours (37). The Furies are sniffers, slitherers, and, in their great choruses, swoopers and stampers who move horizontally to the earth as well as upright against and away from it. Their feet are vindictive (371); they trample (338) and step over those who have trampled or overstepped. That a desire for revenge should be expressed as dancing is not so strange. This is a gut response; some who have been deeply violated would dance on the graves of their enemies. As we have seen, Clytemnestra comes alive with the deaths of her husband and Cassandra. Her movements might approach dance steps to accompany the jubilation she feels.

Their motion is dance and their speech is song—collective rhythmic chant. Their sung "arguments" are characteristic of those with tunnel vision. Singlemindedly they insist on the mere fact of a polluting violation, and have no interest in circumstances, intentions, or subsequent repentance. Their first utterance, a string of repeated words—"get him, get him, get him, get him" (130)—is the first sample of the repetitions, of stanzas and even entire speeches, that we shall hear later in the play. Though they make an argument, their speech is not primarily a medium for exchange and free exploration. Cassandra characterizes them as a "chorus that sounds together" (*choros xumphthongos*, *Ag.*, 1186). Their music is "not of the lyre" (*aphormiktos*, 333); it cannot accompany speech. They ask only rhetorical questions. They don't exchange differing views about those they pursue, and they don't make decisions by counting votes. Their most impressive utterance is the "binding song," and they themselves are called "curses" (417). From time immemorial, there has been no arguing with Furies. But, after emerging into the light at Delphi, they are led to Athens where, by agreeing to participate in a trial—an inquiry—they are certain to be superseded by a new kind of justice, one that will replace dancing and chanting with looking and talking.

The most striking thing about the looks of the Furies is that, although they are not human in form (412) or unequivocally women (48), they are somehow female. Daughters of Mother Night (321), they have no father. Their gender suggests that the desire for hands-on, immediate, private justice may be more characteristic of women than of men. For all her assertiveness and "male strength of heart," Clytemnestra acts as a woman. Women are characterized by attachment—to place, earth, and growing things, to the kin-blood they have carried within and nourished without, to the men they marry, and to the hearths, altars and burial grounds they tend. Their lives are, by nature, inside, dark, and silent, far more dominated by bodies, place, and time than the lives of men. The female Furies are guardians, above all, of those with the "same blood" (*homaimos*, 605). If they have to choose among blood relations, as in this case, mother and child take precedence, for mother and child may be thought literally to have shared blood.

The Olympian pantheon contains male and female gods. In the earlier plays, we have heard much about them. In the *Eumenides*, for the first time, they appear on stage. Apollo and Athena, like the Furies, have *looks*. Apollo's young, upright, shapely body, however, points away from body, away from the past, memory, and attachment to home, family, and place. The play in which he appears begins on the road at Delphi. Apollo and his shrine are not autochthonous to this place. He has succeeded the older female divinities, Earth, Themis, and Phoebe, with the help of a relatively new male god, Zeus, who is now presented as the completion and reconciliation of the conflicting deities in the earlier plays. The appropriation and transformation of place would be unthinkable for the fixed palace, altars, and hearthplaces of Argos. The Pythia's speech points to the resolution of the whole trilogy.[25] Unlike the exclusive private places we have seen thus far, the shrine has a neutral detached feel about it. An international place, it is located at a crossroads traveled by all the Hellenes who worship there; anyone may come to look.

Apollo, the anthropomorphic and emphatically male "prophet of his father, Zeus" (19), is associated with light as opposed to dark, with distanced vision as opposed to attachment and touch, with "speaking out" (*exaudomenos*, L.B., 272) and music of the lyre as opposed to stamping feet and binding songs. Apollo is singular, distinct, individual—and he is no dancer. The principles he will articulate point to a justice of autonomous individuals, separable from their pasts, home grounds, houses, and families. But Orestes cannot be saved at Delphi. The male, public, enlightened detachment suggested by Apollo's looks is inadequate by itself. As we shall see, Apollonian liberation brings its own characteristic dangers, and Aeschylus is fully aware of them. But "Apollo of the ways" is the right god to put Orestes on the road. The next step in the emergence from the age-old cycle of kin revenge and Furies-justice must be the step he takes to Athens. This last detachment from the burdens of his Argos past will make it possible for him eventually to return to Argos as his proper place. But by then the meaning of place, for him and for the Athenian audience that watches these plays will have been transformed.

Athens is clearly different from Argos. The Athenians are mentioned for the first time at the beginning of the *Eumenides* as builders of roads and cultivators of wild land (13–14). Unlike those who are born and die in the inherited Argive *oikos,* Athenians are self-conscious place-*makers*. The community of families at Athens looks outward, focusing on a high public place, the Acropolis, over the citadel. Temples, public buildings and roads, rather than hearth, palace, and cemetery, are their primary places. Their stories focus on their shared goddess; the hearth of her house (669) is open to all. Aegeus and Theseus are mentioned as unproblematic founders of a *city,* as opposed to a family, dynasty. There are no references to legends of incest, child eating, or perverted hospitality in their distant past. The ancient monarchy seems to have given way peacefully to a democracy that invites full citizens to cross the threshold to public life.

As the city becomes the dominant visible place in the eyes of its citizens, it develops a permanent special place in which public judgments are enacted. Accused violators are no longer to be judged and punished in the place deemed appropriate by distant gods or next-of-kin. Clytemnestra's and Orestes' privately staged trials are not appropriate when the whole city must view the case. The place of justice is set off from family dwellings—no one is born, lives, dies, or is buried there—and it is, at last, in full view. It is often said that the court is open and unroofed to avoid polluting any closed building by the presence of a murderer. But the shared, public, on-view nature of the Areopagus is at least as important.[26] The location of the new public court also points to the shift in gender suggested above. The Areopagus is the hill on which male Athenians defeated the female Amazons who

once challenged Theseus's city (685) and were defeated. The justice of
the new court will be primarily male justice.

The trial of the accused takes place in an articulated time as well as
an articulated place. A herald announces the start of the proceedings
and a trumpet marks the beginning of the presentation of evidence. No
longer can the accused be surprised by his accusers. As a result, the
investigation will take time; court justice is less immediate, less swift,
than Furies justice. Although it remembers the past and acts for the
future, it aims to isolate, or frame, a violation in time. In *Agamemnon*,
past and future events merge, prophecies and curses are unspecific
about time, and causation is unclear.[27] In the *Eumenides*, the old
private vendettas, which seem to have no beginning and which can
never come to an end, give way to the public trial, which limits the
control of the past over the future. But the participants must be
assured that institutional justice is permanent and has the authority
that the fixed and age-old hearth had. Although the citizens know that
the Areopagus has a beginning, and is not, like private hearths, eternal,
Athena repeatedly asserts that the court that concludes past conflicts
will retain its authority "for the rest of time" (572).

Like the private "trials" of the first two plays, the public one
requires a *visible* reconstruction of the alleged violation. Clytemnestra
compels Agamemnon to exhibit himself in a symbolic imitation of his
violations, and her son sets her up in the same way. As we have seen,
these reenactments spur the injured reviewer to execute justice—
immediately and with his own hands. Although public trials remove
the staging and execution from the hands of the injured parties, like
the earlier "dramatic" imitations, they, too, re-present the acts of the
past. Just as every drama can be considered a detective story—
Oedipus is the paradigm here—so every trial can be seen as a play, a
drama in which the dialogue consists entirely of questions and an-
swers. Orestes' trial opens with a request for "witnesses and evidence" (*martyria* and *tekmêria*, 485). Athena's invitation to the prose-
cuting Furies to open the case uses the technical legal language that
itself echoes the language of the theater. They are to be the "producers
of the act" (*pragmatos didaskalos*, 584).

Opening statements, as judges and lawyers sometimes instruct modern juries, are like plot summaries or playbill notes in theater programs.
They are meant to orient the audience before the story is reenacted in
the production itself. Prosecutors and advocates, like the Furies and
Apollo, are partly narrators, partly new actors in the spectacle. They
bear witness (485, 594, 609) and link the testimonies of the original

actors and witnesses who review and reenact what they saw, heard, said, and did, often with original or simulated "props" and "costumes." But the locks of hair, fragments of cloth, footprints, and woven nets presented at public trials are evidence not for private recognitions and responses, as in the Atreid graveyard, but for public examination and judgment. Injured parties now bear witness as an alternative to, rather than as a spur to, personal retaliation. In civilized societies, "bearing witness at a public trial becomes a socially sanctioned form of revenge."[28] By restaging the events in question in a public arena, these witnesses formally share what they have seen with several new kinds of spectators.

All-seeing but invisible Zeus, with his scales of justice, is no longer the main witness in this new form of narrated drama. Just as he was behind all acts of Furies-justice in the first two plays, he still backs up and confirms the Athenian proceedings. But Zeus is not the most prominent overseer to whom Athens now looks. Rather, under the supervision of the manifest, bright-eyed goddess Athena, a collective body of mortals witnesses the action and weighs the evidence. Juries look together with those who have been wronged but, unlike Furies, they do not entirely share their point of view. These new witnesses are thus less shortsighted than both the original ones and the Furies who later claim to bear witness. Through the jury, justice becomes, at the same time, both blind and farsighted. Athena says the Athenian juror-judges are the "best" of her citizens (487). But in the play they are not from any particular class, and there is no indication that they are experts in law or anything else. Rather, they represent the city as a whole, as well-informed citizens who directly participate in the administration of justice. They are not set off from the general population by special dress; their looks affirm their representative status. They have known each other before the trial, and, after it, will continue to face each other and their fellow citizens, as well as those whose case they now witness. They are drawn by lot from different families of the polis.[29] Unlike the excluded onlookers and impotent martyr-witnesses of the Argos plays, these Athenian witnesses are not passive spectators; they are charged to *witness* and to *act*. Their view of the reconstructed past will determine the futures of their fellows. Their witnessing will affect their own futures as well, because their jury duty is part of their own political training, a kind of public schooling that teaches them to judge their neighbors as they themselves may someday be judged.[30] It shifts their attention from their private attachments to public concerns. Jurors are neighbors in the fullest sense of the English word: "near," "nigh," and "neigh-bor" may be derived from the same root as "eye."[31] Being a juror means being on view to those who live nearby, and sharing the common business, places—and views—of a city.[32]

By recapitulating the alleged crime in a public place for public witnesses in a public trial, the city passes through the private *oikos* gates to rule about what takes place within. Non-blood now judges and may punish, because all blood is viewed as having been violated. The defiling and rending of household fabrics is no longer a private matter. The whole community has been rent and its fabric must be examined and rewoven. The trial serves as a ritual act to rid the whole community of pollution. Like revenge, it is a ceremonial expiation or cleansing, and a restoration of balance. The sense of communal purification involved in a trial interestingly echoes the origins of the theater. In the beginning, it is conjectured, all members of the community actively prosecuted and expelled a symbolic scapegoat. At some point, some, and finally most, of these active participants became *watchers* of the action, affirming it as ceremonial witnesses. By the end of the *Oresteia*, justice no longer requires an "eye of the house" or "watchdog" Furies, because, in this tribunal, the whole city is now charged by Athena to be a "sentry on the land" (706) and to become effectively vigilant. The whole city becomes a collective Pylades whose official function is to accompany fellow citizens through the gates. No longer reliant on the murky evidence of seers and prophets, the public viewing aims to be clear.

With the advent of public institutional justice, speech and motion, as well as vision, are clarified. Unlike the repeated stalled speeches of the Furies, the discussion of the litigants in court is a dialogue in motion. Though the jurors constitute a kind of "collective mind" for the community, they vote individually. The ordered stepping of the twelve Athenian jurors as they cast their votes provides a striking contrast with the confused speeches and frantic motion of the twelve Argive elders as they try to imagine what is happening behind the Atreid gates, and with the stamping repetitions of the bent-over Furies. In Athena's new court, "all must stand upright" (708). It is sometimes said that the dense, ambiguous, proleptic language in *Agamemnon* is a sign of a rich, but overexcited, undisciplined imagination, as well as of the badly preserved text. But the increasing clarity of diction in the concluding play makes it clear that Aeschylus could write clearly and simply when he wanted to.[33] The emergence of fully public speech in the Athenian trial of Orestes is *meant* to contrast with the silences, curses, and murky claims of kin justice at Argos. Similarly, the great final procession, in which spectators join actors as an entire city walks together to its public hearth, is meant to contrast with the bound paralysis, frantic motion, and vengeful dancing of the first two plays.

The momentous shift in the relationship between family and non-family, which occurs as public institutional justice replaces family justice, is accompanied by a change in the relationship between the citizens of one city and those of other cities. Societies with increased mobility and contact with strangers can no longer depend on family watchdogs to insure justice. In Athens, public courts are entrusted with the vigilance formerly maintained by permanent families attached to one place. The essence of the hearth (*hestia*) which defines a family is its fixity (as in *histêmi*, from "stay, stand").[34] As we have seen, in the first two plays, "foreign" relations consist, on the one hand, of the terrible war with the distant walled city of Troy and, on the other, of personal guest-friendships like those of Agamemnon with Strophius and Odysseus. There is nothing in between. In *Agamemnon* and the *Libation Bearers*, the word *xenos* (stranger, guest) sounds repeatedly. A world of guest-friendships, of relations between friendly foreigners, is overseen by Zeus *xenios*, the "guest/stranger god" (*Ag.*, 61, 362, 748) and *xunestiou*, the "hearth god" (*Ag.*, 704). The violations of this world—Thyestes' feast, the adultery of Paris and Helen, Cassandra's murder, Orestes' murder of his mother and hosts—are all perversions of the intertwined principles of family and hospitality.

The *Eumenides* shifts the focus from hearth and *oikos* to city and more fully developed international relations. Orestes' trial results in a treaty, not between heads of families, but between the *cities* of Argos and Athens. Many political discussions of the play explore the meaning of the alliance in Athenian politics at the time Aeschylus wrote.[35] But its deeper interest lies in the fact that it develops coevally with public institutional justice within the city. Both developments involve a new attitude to what is originally foreign and un-familiar. As the gates of family households open to the community around them, so the gates of the city now open to admit outsiders. The word *xenos* is heard infrequently in the last play, and is not used at all in the last three hundred lines. The jurors and Orestes are referred to as "friend" or "strangers" in a general way. Though the Furies continue to insist on the protection of god, guest, and parents, Zeus is no longer referred to as Zeus *xenios*, but as Zeus *agoraios* (973). The new epithet means "of the marketplace or assembly," and is also associated with courts and forensic activity.

Cosmopolitan Athens, always open to suppliants and foreigners, takes within itself its first official resident aliens, or "metics," the transformed and kindly Eumenides. In the first two plays, Aeschylus uses the word "metic" anachronistically and metaphorically, in connection with *xenos*. In *Agamemnon*, for example, the Atreids are compared to metics (*metoikon*) in the sky (*Ag.*, 57) and are protected by Zeus *xenios*. In the *Libation Bearers*, Orestes is *metoikon* in Phocis, but "all foreigner [*xenon*] forever" to his native Argos (*L.B.*, 683–84). In *Eumenides*, this foreigner is rehabilitated by his host city and then sent home. At the same time, Athena invites the defeated Furies to "live with me" (*xunoikêtôr emoi*, 833), to "share our country" (*khôras metaskhein*, 869), and, having persuaded them to do so, calls them *metoikoi* (1011). In their own last speech, they refer to their status as a *metoikia* (guest-ship, 1017). The play ends by affirming that there will be peace forever between the people of Pallas and their metics (1045). In the concluding procession of the trilogy, the Furies, their looks utterly transformed, march in crimson robes.[36] In the theater of Dionysus, these robes would be recognized as the official costume of real-life metics in Athens. Though they form a recognizable class, transplanted aliens differ from native families or tribes in that they can never be more than a conventionally defined group. They do not come from demes—neighborhoods associated with exclusive tribes—but from other cities. Though Athens eventually formulates special tax, mercantile, and even trial procedures for their kind, they are originally unconnected individuals, relatives only by law. The last play suggests that, in a community where justice has been transferred from kin to city, outsiders can at last "be at home with" (*met-oikeô*) insiders; even foreigners can have a proper place.

But in Aeschylus's theatrical Athens, as well as in his own city, the continued distinction between native citizens and metics indicates a conviction that the distinction between one's own and others should not be utterly obscured. Though Athena's city has no walls and her gates are open to all, the aliens who cross her threshold and dwell within are never completely assimilated.[37] Athena's settlement with her first metics, the Furies, suggests that full enlightenment and total familiarity with what is alien is not her goal. The progressive thrust of the trilogy is more complicated than it might at first seem. Courteous to everyone in her court, Athena facilitates the victory of male Apollo over female Furies, and then turns her, and our, attention back to them. Enlightened and masculine though she may be, she is female enough to recognize that the power of the rational, visible, new court must be supported by another power, the establishment of which she proclaims with as much solemnity as she proclaimed the founding of the Areopagus. The effectiveness of this other power is a function of its being less rational, less visible, less open to the gaze of mortals than the open court on the hillside. In their new abode, the transformed Furies will still be underground. Sitting on their deep thrones, they will remain guardians of the deep-seated passions depicted in the earlier plays. Like judges today, Athena exhorts her citizen-jurors to judge with their minds. But she recognizes the Furies' argument that the "hearts" of the citizens also matter: "Terror is good" (*to deinon eu*) as a control to "keep watch" (*episkopon*) on the heart (517–18). Thus, after the somewhat tinny arguments of Apollo, we hear once again the ringing language of the Furies and Clytemnestra. Even in the enlightened city, the Eumenides retain power over the households, marriages, and generation of human beings (903 ff.). They will continue as watchers, supervisors, sentries, now for the whole city, rather than for separate families. Citizens will retain solemn awe for and bring sacrifices to the new public hearth,[38] which, like the private hearths of old, will be "for all time" (572). Even as she reshapes them into a recognizable civic institution, Athena, like the shapeless Furies earlier in the play, attempts to articulate the importance of shapeless fear and inarticulate wonder as guards against anarchy, tyranny, civil war, and the sickness and blight that accompany them.

So Athena insists on the continued power of the now-resident Eumenides. But there remain questions about the possibility of maintaining this power. Although the vote is close, we surely celebrate the acquittal of the confessed mother-murderer. The dark fears of the first play have given way to steady torchlight. The blood-soaked earth of Argos recedes into the past as we gaze upon a paved city surrounded by fruitful earth. Man-hearted woman and ineffectual men are superseded by "maidens, wives, elder women, in processional" (1027) and manly citizens. And the short-lived *ololugmoi* of the tormented Atreid household are replaced by the communal *ololugmos* of a rejoicing city (1047). At the end of the trilogy, Aeschylus's Athenian audience may have marched in procession out of the theater with the stage Athenians—now, at last, a great crowd—to look back together on their own progressive history. But thoughtful members of that audience— and today's—might sense that, with the triumph of Athens and the successful assimilation of the Furies into a city that makes even foreigners familiar, something has gone out of the world. Despite the colorful procession, the clarified political language of the last play seems flat, less vibrant, less powerful, than that at the start of the trilogy.[39] After Orestes departs, the only humans on stage are a crowd of anonymous Athenians.[40] Compared to Clytemnestra, Agamemnon, and even Aegisthus, these people must feel smaller.

Even the gods seem somehow diminished at the end of the trilogy. This may seem odd, given the development they have apparently undergone. The conflicting, unpredictable, vengeful, invisible, and distant forces of *Agamemnon* are now integrated, articulated, and gathered together— at last, a pantheon. Athena and Apollo walk among mortals; their looks are guides to those who look to them. As civic gods, however, Athena and Apollo, and even Zeus who meets with Moira to sanction the new settlement, have a different feel from "Zeus whatever he may be" (*Ag.*, 160), the awesome, almost ineffable "bestower of power and beauty" (*Ag.*, 356). Apollo's departure, after the ringing farewell to Orestes, goes unremarked,[41] and Athena leaves in procession among the crowd of anonymous Athenians.

Despite their honored status, the divine Furies *have*, in some sense, been put to rest. We feel this as they move off at the end: the word they repeat, *khairete,* means "farewell" in several senses. These once-vengeful dancers and stampers have been taught to walk in procession; once in place, they will sit still on their thrones. In becoming part of the city's foundation, they have also been buried. In the triumph of the cosmopolitan city, being out of sight may dilute rather than enhance their power. Might the new enlightened ways and institutions so successfully take root that the Furies would cease to stir in the earth? The very progression toward rational, liberated human life with its ever-widening horizons, may mean at the same time, the dissipation and even eradication of the very passions and needs that characterize human beings. I mean attachment to private family and place, the sense of self that develops in opposition to others as foreigners, and the insistence on some form of revenge as the only truly satisfying recompense for the violation of this self and what it considers its own.

Apollo's argument for paternal priority is necessary to establish the beginnings of civilized public justice; insofar as it is *detached*, it emphasizes *masculinity*. The notion that the father is the true parent, and the mother only a "stranger" (*xenos*) to his seed,[42] points to estrangement, as well as to extended brotherhood, as essential features of enlightened modernity. The attenuation of the dark blood-attachments depicted in *Agamemnon* and the *Libation Bearers* is evident in the way we ourselves now live. For the most part, we bear babies outside the home, in public institutions, and swaddle them in clothes made by anonymous strangers. We adopt homeless children who do not share our looks; we give them our names, and love them truly as our own. We move repeatedly and reestablish our hearths where jobs are interesting and schools are good. And we have rational legal procedures for reconstituting these hearths and the families around them when they are no longer satisfying. We count "naturalized" foreigners among our citizens. We deal with criminals in a rational, nonviolent way, and keep our own hands clean in the process. We have achieved technological feats undreamed of by the most enlightened Athenians, and, for the most part, we attribute our successes and our failures to ourselves. And when our much-extended lives are over, we rarely bury our dead with each other or in burial places attached to the places we live in. These changes have made possible enormous advances in human life. We owe our health, prosperity, peace, and civility to them, and few of us would choose to live differently. But, as we have suggested, the triumph may be a qualified one.

Apollo's detachment of mother from child and the vote of Athena, the male-supporting goddess, never "fostered in the dark of the womb" (665) but born from the head of Zeus, point to the losses and dangers implicit in the move toward enlightenment depicted in the *Oresteia*. Perhaps the dancing, hysterical prophetess Cassandra, torn from her family and wailing the deaths of Trojan and Atreid children, refused to bear Apollo's child because she sensed something about the implications of his strange combination of overwhelming power and distanced rationality. Could Cassandra, in some dark, unarticulated way, have forseen the tendencies that issue in two twentieth-century trials, one real and one fictional, but each a paradigm for the dilemmas of modern justice?

Apollo's argument about the paternal parent and the mother as stranger to the child in her womb, points far beyond the trial of Clytemnestra's son to the contemporary trial concerning "Baby M." The trial took place in New Jersey in 1987. A "surrogate mother" conceived a child and carried it to term in accordance with a contract she had made with the man who "contributed sperm." After the birth of the baby, she refused to honor the contract, accept her fee, and give up the child to the "father" and his wife, who intended to become the "adoptive mother." The jury had to decide who would receive custody of the baby. The case raised questions about which parent is "most a parent," about whether blood ties matter more than quality of rearing, and a host of other questions raised by the *Oresteia*. Every detail of Baby M's life and that of the adults who created her was exposed to public view. Even her conception, an enlightened, businesslike event, did not take place in the dark. Healthy and wellprovided for, yet detached from the mother who bore her, not yet sure of her name or of the household to which she belonged, she was the subject of a rational lawsuit that could never have a satisfactory resolution.

Camus' *The Stranger* also depicts the direction in which the *Eumenides* might point.[43] The narrator, whose suggestive name is rarely used, is a stranger in a cosmopolitan society where *everyone* seems *xenos*. He lives a hazy existence punctuated only by moments of sharp physical pleasure. He never set eyes on his father, and rarely sees his mother. He doesn't "love" his girl, but is willing to marry her. Like her, his "friends" are accidentally acquired. His work is of no interest, he eats haphazardly, alone or with whoever is there, and he doesn't care whether he lives in Algiers or Paris. His "home" is a rented apartment—he rarely eats there—and his mother dies in an institutional "home" for the aged. Living only in the present, he has no attachments to the past and no care for the future. He does not believe in God or in a life after death.

The trial that sentences him to death for his meaningless murder of an Arab is a judicial arrangement perfectly suited to his way of life: a jury of strangers, voyeuristic, indifferent journalists looking for news for bored readers in another place, witnesses who hardly know the accused, the victim, or each other, and lawyers who abstractly go through the motions of a trial. The dead man is barely evoked in the brightly lit courtroom, and no connections of his are present or mentioned. All we know of these dark Arabs is that, anachronistically in this cosmopolitan world of strangers, they are out to take revenge on a man who's insulted the sister of one of them. Evidently the Furies are still alive for them. At first, Meursault feels some interest in his trial; he has never witnessed one before. But during the trial he says he "was barely conscious of" who or where he was. He feels as though he is being "scrutinized" by himself, and never catches the eye of the girl who wants to marry him. A stranger at his own trial, he feels like a "gate crasher" and "off the map," and finds it incongruous that he should be sentenced in the name of the "French people"; "why not the Chinese or German people?" he wonders. The sentence of death will be carried out by an efficient machine; no people are mentioned, and the guillotine reminds him of a shining laboratory instrument. In this world of rootless, passionless, unconnected strangers, the sentence of execution "in some public place" also seems an incongruous anachronism. The murderer never regrets his murder, only the anticipated loss of the immediate pleasures of his flat, day-to-day life. He is convicted largely on distorted "evidence" about his mother's funeral. But, as the nameless prosecutor says, there is a "psychological" connection between the murder and Meursault's distance from his mother. The prosecutor does not realize, as we must, that the court, the journalists, the police, the Arabs, Algiers, Paris, and he himself form a coherent whole. It is a long way from the deaths of Agamemnon, Aegisthus, and Clytemnestra to the deaths of Meursault's mother, the nameless Arab, and Meursault himself, but a thread runs between them.

The acquittal of Orestes and the victory of Apollo is rightly celebrated by Athenian and modern viewers alike. But we no longer live with Eumenides under the ground, and there is little in our lives to remind us that these guardians are ever-watchful. Having made the choice for Athens over Argos, however, we can be mindful that there are other choices yet to be made. What we have learned from Argos, Clytemnestra, and the Furies may clarify alternatives as we arrange the day-to-day workings of our political institutions. Perhaps the choice for enlightenment need not lead inevitably to Baby M in the spotlight and the Stranger dazed by the Algerian sun.

Part Four:
Making Justice Visible: Trials and Tragedies

Present-minded goddess that she is, Athena's concerns are primarily with the *founding* of the city's court and hearth. Nothing is said about the particular judicial procedures that Athens will follow. The last part of this chapter will explore institutional arrangements that are not discussed explicitly in Aeschylus's plays, but that can contribute to keeping alive, even in enlightened times, something of what the Furies stand for. Some of these institutions—courts and prisons—are recognizably political, and our discussion of them can be about ourselves. Just as Furies retain their power by being out of sight yet not invisible, so, perhaps, in the apprehension of suspects, and in the trial and punishment of convicted violators, a political community can attain the right combination of restricted view and visibility. The effect of what a community watches can also be judged from another institution found there—the theater. To think about the tragic drama as a civic teacher, we must return to Athens, for the theater in our times is not so recognizably a political institution as it was in Aeschylus's city. Our consideration of both judicial and theatrical arrangements will focus once more on what we have learned from Aeschylus's trilogy about what human beings need to *see.*

In Argos, people are bound by their looks. Kin resemblances are clear, families keep watch over their own, and citizens recognize each other. In larger, more mobile, cosmopolitan societies where family is no longer the primary influence, it is less likely that people will be on view to each other, either before or after violations are committed. Crime in big cities is increased by anonymity and by tolerance for unconventional behavior and insults. Unfamiliar people, who don't recognize each other's looks, are more likely to look the other way when crimes are committed and when those who commit them are punished.

How should a political community *begin* to deal with those who "trample on the right?" Clytemnestra, Orestes, and the Furies arrange swiftly to isolate their apprehended victims behind closed doors. They reveal the "punishment" only after it has been accomplished. After the *Eumenides,* the pursuit, apprehension, and punishment of violators is out in the open, visible to all. The initial effect may be one of public awe, but eventually the visible administration of justice may become less dramatic, and more businesslike. Ironically, the public process may become so routine that it might even retreat once more behind closed doors—not of private houses, but of impersonal institutions. In our times, apprehended suspects are usually detained until legal proceedings can be initiated. A community must decide whether the movements of such suspects should be visible or out of view to their fellow citizens. For example, should local jails and court houses be located where they and their activities can be observed by ordinary citizens on their way to school, work, or the post office? Most of us are understandably disturbed as we pass an officer hustling a handcuffed suspect out of a wagon into the sheriff's office. The suspect may hide his face and we try not to stare. Nevertheless, we have taken note of each other, and have been reminded of the sort of community we live in. Both the need to notice and our mutual reluctance to look indicate the connection between public morality and shame. Recent technology has made it possible to conduct bail hearings by closed-circuit television between judges' chambers and local jails. This eliminates expensive and time-consuming transporting and guarding of suspects between jails and courtrooms. Paradoxically, however, the new video equipment reduces the *public* visibility of the judicial process. Bail hearings become a private, but now impersonal, matter between officials and the accused, instead of a public event visible to injured parties and all interested citizens.

The importance of the visibility of court trials has already been emphasized in our consideration of the *Eumenides*. The play suggests that, at his trial, the convicted violator must face his accusers and punishers and acknowledge that he will pay the consequences of his violation with his eyes open. He, too, sees justice done. Unlike Agamemnon, Helen, Clytemnestra, and Aegisthus, he knows that although he once acted as if no one were watching, the eyes of others are now upon him. If a visibly staged public trial is important, perhaps something may be lost—from a civic point of view—when we resort to more efficient, behind-the-scenes plea bargaining to speed up the judicial process. Is it always better for speedy justice to take precedence over visible justice? When civil trials replace kin revenge, perhaps the community can try to remember how important it is for kin and unrelated citizens to witness the proceedings. Surviving kin are usually the most visible and vocal spectators at murder trials. In court literature it is commonplace to hear the most law-abiding, peaceable citizens declare, "If I see justice done, I'll be satisfied. If they let him off, I'll murder him with my own hands."

The 1987 French trial of the Nazi officer Klaus Barbie had as its main end the face-to-face confrontation of this murderer with his victims. Barbie's refusal to remain present at his trial deprived his victims of the main satisfaction that the trial could, at this late date, hold out to them. Newspaper reports referred to his walkout as a "new escape." It was clear that forcing the "butcher" to face his victims at last as human beings among other human beings, and to acknowledge his crimes, was at least as important as any technical conviction that the trial might produce. The same point is often made by those who object to plea bargaining. In 1993, a trial was canceled because the defendant, a former priest accused of dozens of cases of sexual abuse of children, had pleaded guilty. The judge was persuaded to allow all of the now-adult victims to confront the defendant at the sentencing and to make statements, which were widely reported in the press. The importance of visual confrontation is a recurrent theme in most discussions of crime and punishment—from detective fiction to trial lawyers' advice books to books about trials.[44] Unlike the "trials" of Thyestes, Helen, Agamemnon, and Clytemnestra at one extreme, and of the Stranger at the other, our trials aim at eye contact,[45] but in the presence of confirming witnesses. This mutual seeing is an element of revenge justice that must be transformed in public courts. But should it be entirely eliminated?

The looking of jurors must also be considered. In Athens the entire citizen population routinely served as judges in trials. In large modern cities, few citizens ever serve on juries or even attend trials. It is also unlikely that those who do will have seen each other in other contexts before a trial. As we have seen, the trial is set in a "frame"; it is a contained action articulated from the past and from the future. But should we not be careful lest the frame distance the crime too much from the life that contains it? Jury service is a rare experience in the life of a modern citizen, often confined to a few brief days. Jurors are not routinely aware of the final disposition of cases. When they acquit, they rarely hear of a future conviction. Their job is to judge the accused, not to solve a case or satisfy the injured. When they give guilty verdicts, they are often unaware of the punishment that follows, because judges often sentence after a trial. Might their failure to see the trial through to its very end diminish the gravity of the jurors' judgments? They may look together during the trial, but do they feel that they continue to be a community after it? After a recent trial, one jury member reported that the jurors "all said we'd be in touch, and maybe get together again. I guess that won't happen, but when we were leaving the courtroom we all said we'd try."[46] Is it possible for justice to become *too* impersonal?

The looking *of* juries will be effective, as we have seen, only if it is accompanied by carefully arranged public looking *at* and *with* juries. As a modern judge instructs the jurors:

> Not only must juries exonerate the innocent and convict the guilty, they must *appear* to be doing that. If the public loses confidence that juries are rationally settling violent disputes between society and those accused of offending it, personal acts of vigilantism, revenge, lynchings, and riots are not far-fetched consequences. [47]

Public observation and supervision have always been essential features of jury trials. In free societies, public officials, news reporters, and interested private citizens are expected, and even encouraged, to witness the proceedings. This last group is especially interesting. On the one hand, these people observe because it is in their interest to supervise and monitor this public business. But this group has also always contained people who find the "dramas" they witness there interesting, and entertaining. These retirees, students, housewives, and other citizens, attend courtroom dramas in person. Working people, who cannot do this, get their reports through the media, which, like juries, serve as watchdogs against injustice in modern democracies.

It has been suggested that the routine televising of trials, like other public events, would contribute to public interest and care for the law. Once again, however, experience with modern video technology suggests the drawbacks of this suggestion. Consider the theatricalization of televised congressional hearings, interestingly confused by many viewers with trials. Consider also the popularity of television shows such as "The People's Court," "Divorce Court," and "L.A. Law." Their appeal ranges from curiosity about the rich and famous, to the desire to make one's own judgment and compare it with that of a real judge, to identification with the characters, to an interest in psychology. Like many soap opera fans who confuse the fictions they watch with real life, these television viewers are often unclear about whether they are watching trials, reports of trials, or theater, especially since the "plots" vary in how scripted they are.[48]

This kind of slippage can be extremely dangerous in a community whose institutional system of justice depends on the ability of its citizens to see clearly, and to make distinctions. When public looking—in the theater or in the courts—degenerates into private voyeurism, both civic and private virtue are likely to decline. Through television the public now has access to a greater view than ever before in human history. We see to the far limits of the earth and into the most private situations. But this viewing is essentially private. There can be no eye contact between watcher and watched; and, in the case of trials, the consciousness of being exposed to millions of viewers would be too abstract to have the effect that personal, face-to-face, or more local, shaming has. Finally, the millions watch in private homes. Televised trials are like televised Thanksgiving parades and televised New Year's parties; the TV does not allow citizens to look *together*. Televised trials[49] provide easy access to what is usually behind the closed doors of private homes and even of public courts. But televised trials are also observed from behind closed doors. Television takes us through the gates whose penetration the *Oresteia* dramatizes, but it may not provide an effective middle ground between private and public. Is a media public—now mostly a television public—enough? The *Oresteia* suggests that human beings require a community that is more immediately felt and visible.[50]

The same concern for public vision might help decide what *punish-*

ment is appropriate when a suspect has been judged guilty.[51] For example, visible punishment within the community might be preferable to banishment. Homer tells of people who have killed and are expelled from their communities in order to avoid blood feuds. By turning the killer into an invisible outsider, continual bloodshed is avoided and the surviving kin may be spared the constant offense of having to view the violator, a difficult sight even if there has been some recompense. But exiling the killer may be just another way of averting one's eyes and looking away. The banishing community shows him for what he is, but then makes him invisible. Banishment may punish the violator by taking away home and identity; but eventually, if he no longer sees his home place, the violator may develop satisfying attachments to a new home.

As we have seen, the Furies both drive the offender from home, and keep him bound to it. For those who have been violated and remain in place, even an effective banishment ceremony may fail to satisfy. They may require visible punishment within the bounds of the place they once shared with the violator. We might remember the Chorus's description of Helen here: though in exile, she left a "phantom vision" in Argos and reduced those she shamed to less than their former selves. To become whole again, Clytemnestra needs to *see* Agamemnon's punishment. She and Orestes retaliate in the very places their victims offended them; the justice of it pleases. The worldwide pursuit of former Nazis (like Klaus Barbie) who pose no continued threat indicates clearly that visible punishment is more important than mere removal. Punishment at home keeps the convicted criminal as an example before the eyes of other would-be criminals, but it aims at more than utilitarian deterrence. It speaks to those who do live by the expectations and bonds of the community. It affirms that attachment to community, like ties to a natural family, is permanent.[52] Visible punishment in place is a way of continuing to recognize the Furies in an enlightened, civilized community.

Civilization cannot accept Clytemnestra's savage pleasure in the blood of her husband, or allow the satisfactions of those who would dance round the gallows or electric chair. But should civilization entirely suppress the passionate desire to *see* justice executed? Perhaps the punishment of convicted criminals, like their trials, should not be removed too far from sight. It is true that prison walls, like accused criminals in handcuffs, are disturbing sights to some law-abiding citizens. Furthermore, some say they take up valuable space and present a danger to those living near them. It is easy to appreciate the reasons for the distant removal of the place of punishment, as well as the place of judgment, from the ordinary law-abiding life of a community. Less obvious are the reasons that might argue against removal. Large, isolated prisons make rehabilitation of convicted violators less likely. Small-town jails were intended as temporary holding places until all but the most incorrigible detainees could be reintegrated into the community. Remaining on view to law-abiding citizens, jailed violators were not thoroughly severed from their past identities. For the most part, they *looked* like themselves. Huge penitentiaries in distant locations, however, are often pens to keep society's outcasts, rather than rehabilitation centers, as they were originally intended to be, for those who had become "penitent." Such places tend to reduce prisoners to faceless nonpersons in uniform, or, worse, to beasts. [53] The change in their looks, however, may not shame them into reform—as it might do if others could see them—but is often merely a means to control. Also unclear is the effect such prisons have on those who incarcerated these outcasts. Except for violent outbreaks, once they are out of sight, they are, for the most part, out of mind. To the larger community, the changed looks and reduced lives of inmates are invisible. They are, in effect, banished, but without the advantages of banishment. "Prison awareness" programs attempt to bring volunteers to prison inmates for quasi-social contacts. But these programs involve very few people, and the motives of and effects on those who participate are unclear. Teenagers from high-crime areas are sometimes given prison tours in hopes that such sight-seeing will discourage would-be violators.[54] But does it have this effect? More important, the distant location and euphemistic names of these "correction facilities" may fail to satisfy those who have been violated and to remind those who live with them that justice has been and is being done. Once again, "justice must not only be done; it must be seen to be believed."[55] Perhaps it is not too wasteful of space and too offensive to civilized sensibilities for native Chicagoans and out-of-town sight-seers to look down from the Sears Tower and see, in one direction, municipal buildings, and, in the other, prisoners exercising on a nearby roof. We should also consider the outside life that might be observed from captivity by these prisoners, and, more likely, by those in the jail of a smaller town. Might they be more likely to return to law-abiding lives than Camus' Stranger, who sees only an empty patch of sky from his cell, or than a prisoner in an isolated state pen? Perhaps freedom, too, must be on view.

The importance of visibility in apprehending, trying, and incarcerating violators, might suggest, for some violations, more visible punishments than incarceration. This does not mean, of course, public torture or executions, or even milder exposure to public censure like stocks or dunkings. The hanging of a pickpocket has often been observed to be the most inviting and lucrative opportunity for other pickpockets, and experience has long shown that turning the execution of justice into public spectacle is as bad for the souls of the punishers as it is for the souls and bodies of those punished. Cesare Beccaria, the influential eighteenth-century opponent of capital punishment and public torture, nevertheless suggests an advantage of penal servitude: "it inspires terror in the spectator more than in the sufferer. Public punishment of lesser crimes, which are closer to men's hearts, will make an impression which, while deterring them from these, deter them from the graver crimes."[56] Unlike Orestes, who is acquitted and returns to his city looking like himself, the first guilty murderer in the Bible is sentenced to a life of fugitive wandering (there are not yet distinct communities) and of visible shame. The mark of Cain deters other murderers and, for Cain himself, is an indelible sign of his separation, even after he builds his city. Thinking about Cain does not suggest the return to public excoriation of scapegoats, but it does invite reconsideration of the place of shame in civilized communities. For lesser crimes than Cain's and Orestes', might devices like taggings, bumper stickers, newspaper confessions and apologies, and other visible publication of the trials and punishments of legally convicted violators be more effective than banishing them from our sight?

And what if one concludes that, in some cases, capital punishment, the complete and permanent removal from the sight of fellow human beings (Hades is Greek for "unseen"), is the appropriate sentence? It seems right that executioners be anonymous, blindfolded, masked, and not act singly, so that public justice in the name of the community may be done impersonally, and so that no new Clytemnestra will bloody her hands. Recent accounts of the desire of surviving relatives, curious journalists, professors of sociology, and voyeuristic or bloodthirsty fellow citizens to witness executions make it clear that such acts must *never* be public spectacles—either live or on television. This last suggestion is another example of how modern video technology could pervert civic visibility. Yet the gravity of an execution demands that it not be done completely behind closed doors. It has been suggested that one way to allow an enlightened community to observe such a dark event would be for executions to be witnessed officially by community representatives—perhaps elected legislators—just as representative juries witness the trials that convict such violators.[57] One may well be reluctant to embrace capital punishment as the only appropriate response to the most heinous crimes. But it does seem that especially those who retain doubts about it should advocate, instead, public and visible ways to deal with violators of the laws. For if civilized, institutional justice fails to satisfy in the ways we have been considering, private revenge is likely to supplement it where the public institutions are felt to be inadequate. Or, just as bad, as I have been suggesting, human beings who have lost the passions that require satisfaction may cease to demand redress.

At the end of the *Oresteia,* a crucial step has been taken. The Athenian trial provides the solution, or the remedy, to the age-old horror in Argos. But the difficult political decisions about arraignments, trials, punishments, and other proceedings concerning violators are yet to be worked out. Orestes' story and that of his family suggest that, when juries replace Furies, the judicial arrangements should pay special attention to the way things look.

Let us conclude by returning to Athens, a city that paid close attention to what its citizens could and should see. Its own looks, its public buildings, assemblies, courts, festivals, processions, and, above all, its *theater* all attest to this concern for the visible in civic life. In the *Oresteia,* Athena persuades the Furies that they will be accorded permanent reverence in their new residence. The public hearth will be a visible focus for what they stand for. But unlike other divinities on the Acropolis, the Eumenides themselves will not be visible. Their continuing power and the awe they inspire has something to do with their not being accessible to the sight of mortals. On the other hand, as they fear at first and as I have suggested above, their hiddenness may work the other way. Their place beside the house of Erechtheus is under the ground; the temple shines in the sunlight, but they themselves are out of sight. Athena suggests that the Athenians will know that they are there, unseen, but ever-vigilant. But she makes no arrangements for future generations of Athenians, born under the blessing of these dread goddesses, to *behold* them or to *imagine* what is out of sight. It is left to Aeschylus regularly to exhume the Furies [58] in the theater of Dionysus, and to bring the Athenians *face-to-face* with them and with the Argive events that led to their taking up residence in Athens. Wise goddess though she is, Athena, like Apollo, does not dance. She stages trials and processions, but not tragedies. Aeschylus knows that full human beings require tragedies.

From the beginning, I have called attention to the theatrical aspects of private justice, and suggested analogies between the public court and the public theater. Trials and tragedies both invite a whole community of conforming citizens to viewings of stories that contradict and undermine civic life. Both exhibit what is usually out of view: suppressed or deviant behavior that violates the boundaries enforced by the city. Citizen-spectators look, listen, and judge the protagonists in both judicial and theatrical recapitulations of past events. But there are differences as well.

The courts display criminal violations as wrong. Though their justice differs from the old Furies-justice by considering intentions and circumstances as well as deeds, their stance toward the crimes they view is unequivocally negative. In the realm of the political and moral, citizen-spectators may pity the plaintiffs and even identify with a condemned criminal, but they know that the events they view are entirely regrettable. Defendants and advocates attempt to arouse pity, and trial lawyers rehearse witnesses and defendants—their actors—so as to achieve the desired effect on the spectators. But the first aim of the court is to inspire not pity, but fear. This is the *phobos* of which the Furies speak, and which Athena insists must be retained in the enlightened legal system that replaces them. The word is derived from *phebomai*, "to be put to flight." Like those who behold the Furies, those who witness the reconstructions of terrible acts in a trial will "flee" from similar ones. Though a trial, like a play, is a framed representation, the action imitated there is entirely continuous with the real life that comes before and after it. Thus, a writer-juror in a murder trial muses:

> It was like a morality play, with all the different acts, all performed on the stage of the courtroom with all the different players. And we the jurors were part of the cast. But the judge's charge shook me into realizing that this wasn't just a play. The Collins woman really bled, and Rafshoon's life really was on the line.[59]

When possible, the actors play themselves, and jurors and spectators judge them as such. Though trials are punctuated by beginnings and ends, and participants do somehow shift roles at the end of them, there is not an abrupt "breaking of frame" at the conclusion as there is with a play.[60]

The looking of spectators in the theater of Dionysus is somewhat different. The pity and fear that are inspired there contain a dimension not included in the pity and fear of the law courts. Although theater spectators, too, are invited to look and judge, they do not deliberate. Their judgments of reenacted past deeds will not have immediate political consequences for real people. Thus, although it is like a trial in that it takes place in a carefully arranged civic context, this looking is not exclusively political; it is not for the sake of action. Although the story is about themselves, and though stage-Athenians and live-Athenians may merge as they leave the theater, the events seen there are more framed than those revealed in a trial. The tragedies make visible the terrible things—*deina*—that enlightened cities suppress: the rapes, parricides, adulteries, child-eating, defiled corpses, and passionate revenges that have been overcome in the progress toward civilization. In the theater, all viewers stand like Pylades and like jurors, at the gates or on the threshold, and look within. But their view of such terrible things will be more complex than that of court jurors who aim merely—and rightly—to eliminate them.

In the *Eumenides*, Clytemnestra and Orestes and the whole Argive experience that they bring to Athens are, like the Furies, "terrible to speak and terrible for the eyes to see."(34) They remind us of Sophocles' Oedipus in the Athenian grove of the Furies: "terrible to see, terrible to hear" (*deinos men horan deinos de kluein, Oed. Col.*, 141). As the staged Athenians in the plays grant Orestes the gift of his life, and Oedipus the gift of his death, the enlightened city *receives* a gift in return. For in Orestes, as in Oedipus, they may see, without risking their own destruction, what is usually out of view to civilized cities. And they may learn from what they see. Similarly, Aeschylus's fellow Athenians, looking together in the theater of Dionysus, may experience something of the elemental instincts that are as essential to their humanity as are the rational arrangements that have superseded them. In facing these buried things, they may be reminded that the institutions of the civilized city must not forget the passions revealed in these old stories. Even enlightened citizens do—or should—demand that impersonal institutions be as vigilant in apprehending, trying, and punishing violators as next-of-kin once were. Male distance should not obliterate female insistence that it is right to defend—and, maybe, even to kill for—what is one's own by nature. Nonrational attachments to what is our own, and the need for some form of visible retaliation, should not be completely disregarded, even as they are contained by our more orderly impulses. Public punishment, with its eyes on the future, aims at deterrence and rehabilitation. But should it not remember that the past—somehow—requires visible revenge? Our institutional arrangements should not become so antiseptic and abstract that we lose sight of our first—in all senses of the word—demands of justice.

The linear progress that produced the city's rational life is celebrated by enlightened Athens in the midst of a festival that deliberately shatters this way of life and returns, somehow, to first things. The nighttime processions, shadowy, formless masquerades, and the ever-felt presence of Dionysus throughout the festival, make it clear that this is the time for reaffirming nonpolitical passions. The spectators in the theater may have been seated by tribe, and the Dionysiac dithy-rambs were tribal presentations, underlining the family attachments that other civic arrangements attempted to weaken. The Assembly did not meet during the Great Dionysia and so no trials were held. Hard as it is to imagine, convicted prisoners were released on bail during the festival period.[61]

At the core of the festival is the *Oresteia,* which, while inviting its viewers to celebrate the progressive triumph of the court at Athens, first forces them to dwell in the house of Atreus, to come face-to-face with Dionysus, not as Apollo's peaceful partner (*Eum.,* 26), but unassimilated and raw. It is no accident that the Furies so often remind us of the Dionysian maenads in Euripides' *Bacchae.*[62] The songs and dances of cyclic revenge are heard once more, not merely as the ancient echoes of rightly suppressed barbarity, but as the eternal reverberations of what makes us human. Although the *Oresteia* ends with the possibility of the resolution of human tragedy in political solutions, Aeschylus himself, in the theater, reintroduces the possibil-ity of tragedy into the city. In their subsequent deliberations in assem-blies and courts, the Athenians' face-to-face view of Clytemnestra and the Furies will be as formative as the detached reasoning of Apollo, Athena, and the jurors. In addition to Athena's rational arrangements for maintaining fear of invisible powers under the hill, Aeschylus orchestrates sheer terror at the looks of things. By reenacting the story of the House of Atreus, the playwright thus supplements the political job of the courts, and completes the unfinished work of the goddess. Together, Athena and Aeschylus might make it possible for Athenians to look together and see justice done. And, perhaps, the *Oresteia* can also give some guidance to us.

Notes

1. C. S. Lewis's unfinished story, "After Ten Years" in *The Dark Tower and Other Stories* (New York, 1977), captures Menelaus's mixed yearnings for

love, revenge, and dignity as he recaptures Helen at Troy. Note the emphasis in Lewis's story on Menelaus's visions, Helen's looks, their eye contact, and the discrepancy between Agamemnon's victory and Menelaus's loss.

2. John Jones, *On Aristotle and Greek Tragedy* (New York, 1962), p. 87; Amy A. Kass, "The Homecoming of Penelope" (unpublished lecture), University of Chicago, 1981; Anne Lebeck, *The Oresteia: A Study in Language and Structure* (Cambridge, Mass., 1971), pp. 74–86.

3. J. Huizinga, Homo Ludens: *A Study of the Play Element in Culture* (Boston, 1955), p. 80; Pierre Chantraine, *Dictionaire Etymologique de la Langue Grecque* (Paris, 1968), vol. 1–2, p. 284.

4. William C. Scott, *Musical Design in Aeschylean Theater* (Hanover, N. H., 1984), p. 7.

5. Colin McLeod, "Politics and the *Oresteia*," *Journal of Hellenic Studies* 102 (1982), p. 142.

6. There are twelve speeches.

7. "There is no satisfaction in vengeance unless the offender has time to realize who it is that strikes him, and why retribution has come upon him," says the avenger in Arthur Conan Doyle's "A Study in Scarlet," *The Complete Sherlock Holmes* (Garden City, N.Y., 1930), p. 79.

8. A similar revival is claimed by a character in a story described by Susan Jacoby, *Wild Justice* (New York, 1983), p. 56.

9. In the *Bacchae*, for example. See chapter 2.

10. Oliver Taplin, *The Stagecraft of Aeschylus* (Oxford, 1977), p. 328. See also Anthony Podlecki, *The Political Background of Aeschylean Tragedy* (Ann Arbor, 1966), p. 68.

11. See George Thomson, *Aeschylus and Athens* (New York, 1968), p. 247.

12. Taplin, pp. 331–32.

13. The text is corrupt.

14. Fustel de Coulanges, *The Ancient City* (Garden City, N.Y., 1956), p. 27.

15. Jones, p. 85.

16. Fustel, p. 37.

17. Taplin admits this possibility, but argues that a side entry was more likely.

18. Richard Kuhns, *The House, the City, and the Judge: The Growth of Moral Awareness* in The Oresteia (New York, 1962), pp. 27, 31, 50; Thomas G. Rosenmayer, *The Art of Aeschylus* (Berkeley, 1982), pp. 297–98.

19. Fustel, pp. 34–35.

20. Lebeck, pp. 23, 47–48, 159.

21. Robert Fagles and W. C. Stanford, in the introduction to Fagles' translation (New York, 1982), also speak of the middle play as a "new attempt to penetrate the massive walls" (p. 64). Thomson argues that Orestes' situation parallels that of an initiate in the Eleusinian mysteries, who, after an extended *agôn*, becomes part of the visionary company. In the *Libation Bearers*, the contest is carried out under the supervision of his friend. The Chorus is

Seeing Justice Done

"admitted into the secret of the plot" but Chorus members may not "behold" its execution. Pylades is to accompany him into the palace, "to stand over him and watch" (p. 253). Of course, the triumphant echoes of the mysteries in this scene are soon reversed in despair (p. 257). Fagles and Stanford also emphasize the rites of passage and initiation themes (pp. 68, 69, 86).

22. Taplin, pp. 357–58.

23. R. P Winnington-Ingram, "The Role of Apollo in the *Oresteia*," *The Classical Review* (July, 1933), p. 100.

24. Court Theater, University of Chicago, Autumn, 1986.

25. Lebeck, p. 142.

26. The *Iliad*. XVIII. 504. The primitive court on Achilles' shield takes place in the "sacred circle."

27. Lebeck, p. 36. See also Jacqueline de Romilly, *Time in Greek Tragedy* (Ithaca, N.Y., 1968), chap. 3.

28. Jacoby, pp. 354–58.

29. Kuhns, p. 66.

30. On American juries and civic education, see Alexis de Tocqueville, *Democracy in America,* vol. I, chap. 16.

31. *Webster's New World Dictionary of the American Language, College Edition* (Cleveland and New York, 1960), pp. 983, 991.

32. I present, as Aeschylus does, the best case for the jury. See A. R. W. Harrison, *The Law of Athens*. vol. II (Oxford, 1968–71), and Richard Garner, *Law and Society in Classical Athens* (London, 1987) for descriptions of the actual workings of courts and juries at the time Aeschylus lived.

33. Rosenmayer, p. 104.

34. Fustel, p. 61.

35. Podlecki, pp. 81 ff.; K. J. Dover, "The Political Aspects of Aeschylus' *Eumenides,*" *Journal of Hellenic Studies* 77 (1957), pp. 230–37; Franz Stoessl, "Aeschylus as a Political Thinker," *American Journal of Philology* (73, no. 2, 1952), 113–39; "Political" is more broadly understood by McLeod (note 5 above) and by J. Peter Euben, "Justice and the *Oresteia,*" *American Political Science Review* 76, no. 1 (1982), pp. 22–23.

36. Thomson, p. 275.

37. See chapter 2, for a fuller discussion of the festival arrangements.

38. Kuhns, pp. 87–88.

39. Euben, p. 31; Lebeck, pp. 131–32, 135–36.

40. Richmond Lattimore, Introduction, *Oresteia* (Chicago, 1953), p. 31.

41. Winnington-Ingram, "Orestes and Apollo," in *Studies in Aeschylus* (Cambridge, 1983), p. 147.

42. See Lebeck, pp. 114–30, on words used for parents and children in the *Libation Bearers*.

43. Walter Berns, *For Capital Punishment* (New York, 1979), pp. 156–63, says the novel is a "brilliant description of our world" as Camus saw it, but uses the novel itself to argue against the anti-capital-punishment position

Camus espoused in "Reflections on the Guillotine," *Resistance, Rebellion and Death,* trans. Justin O'Brien (New York, 1960), pp. 220, 222. My summary of the novel emphasizes the relations among the themes of attachment, visibility, and public justice as the Oresteia invites us to consider them. I have used the Stuart Gilbert translation of *The Stranger* (New York, 1946).

44. Seymour Wishman, *Anatomy of a Jury: The System on Trial* (New York, 1986), p. 102. See note 7.

45. Thus, the serious architect of a courtroom considers the effects of round or rectangular rooms and the angles at which witnesses, defendant, and jury face each other. See Allan Greenberg, "Selecting a Courtroom Design," *Judicature* 59, no. 9 (1976), 422–28.

46. Wishman, p. 250.

47. Wishman, p. 43; Jacoby, p. 362.

48. Michael Ryan, "They Tell It to This Judge on TV," *Parade,* July 5, 1987, pp. 8–9. The ultimate confusion is found in the real-life trial of Joan Collins, a soap actress whom the same audience had watched take the stand as a TV character in the fictional murder trial of her TV husband. See Trustman Sanger, "Soaking Up the Summertime Soaps," *The Washington Post, August 2,* 1987, C 1–3.

49. In 1991, CBS became the first network to film real courtroom trials as a prime-time series. "Verdict" predictably focused on especially dramatic trials with much human interest and little legal complexity. Also in 1991, the Courtroom Television Network, an all-trial cable channel, began offering all-day viewing of real trials with commentary. It is not surprising that, in 1993–1994, Court TV devoted extensive coverage to trials about the parental custody of a teenager who, at birth, was sent home from the hospital with the wrong parents, and to the trials of defendants accused of sexual mutilation by a spouse, and of the murder of parents. Such television programs seem to risk transforming civic events of the highest seriousness into entertainment that might provide an alternative to other TV dramas, soap operas, talk shows, or the news.

50. See chapter 2 for a discussion of public and private viewing.

51. Readers familiar with Michel Foucault's *Discipline and Punish* (New York, 1979) will find that many of its themes overlap with those of this chapter. These include the judging, transporting, incarcerating, punishing, and rehabilitation of convicted criminals. Especially interesting is his emphasis on visibility and public ceremony (the French title of the book is *Surveiller et Punir; Naissance de la prison*). However, his concern for strategies of power makes him concentrate on two models at the expense of a third. He describes the sovereign monarch who controls unindividuated masses through public shows of power; he also explores the modern use of democratic, administrative surveillance to control individual violators, especially after they are apprehended and are subject to comprehensive observation in incarcerating institutions. But he is less concerned with the continual *mutual* viewing that modern

democratic institutions might aim at. This is the kind of politics that interests me here. Some of his scholarly followers, especially some of those interested in the Renaissance and in Shakespeare's politics, also seem to reduce all political activity to shows of power.

52. Andrew Oldenquist, "The Case for Revenge," *The Public Interest,* no. 82 (Winter, 1986), p. 78.

53. Wishman, p. 13, calls attention to the use of the word "feeding" for prisoners' meals. See also Camus, "Guillotine," pp. 143–44.

54. Jacoby, p. 275.

55. Beachcomber (J. B. Morton) *The Oxford Book of Aphorisms,* chosen by John Gross (Oxford, 1983), p. 111.

56. Cesare Beccaria, *On Crimes and Punishments,* trans. Henry Paolucci (New York, 1963), pp. 48, 57.

57. Berns, pp. 187–88.

58. It was the practice not to have more than one performance of a tragedy. However, after Aeschylus died, as a special honor to him his plays were apparently permitted to be repeated. This way of honoring the civic playwright was itself a civic act. Though Aeschylus could not literally be responsible for this, the repeat performances of the *Oresteia,* I shall suggest, fulfill one of the purposes for writing the drama to begin with.

59. Wishman, pp. 249–50.

60. See Erving Goffman, *Frame Analysis* (New York, 1974) for an exhaustive analysis of "framing." On the ends of trials, see Wishman, p. 250.

61. See chapter 2 for a fuller discussion of the festival.

62. See chapter 2. Also William Whallon, "Why Is Artemis Angry?" *American Journal of Philology* 82 (1961), pp. 84–88; and William Whallon, "Maenadism in the *Oresteia,*" *Harvard Studies in Classical Philology* 68 (1946), pp. 317–27.

2

Looking Together in Athens

Euripides' *Bacchae* and the Festival of Dionysus

Looking at the *Bacchae,* we do not see all that Euripides meant to show, for the text is incomplete. How is it that just as we come to the most terrible parts, after Agave has exhibited the dismembered corpse of her son and invited the Chorus to eat of the feast, how is it that just here so much of the text is lost to us? Scholars speculate about torn manuscripts and they scour ancient citations, hoping to recover missing lines. Editors labor to piece together sections from a twelfth-century play called *Christus Patiens,* parts of which are cribbed from the *Bacchae.* But we who read the play or watch it in the theater realize, as we approach the end, that we can hardly bear to look, hardly bear to hear. What the *Bacchae* shows is obscene; what it says is unspeakable. Nevertheless, we feel compelled to see what it shows, to say what it means.

This essay is a suggestion about a kind of poetic justice. Might the mangled corpse have resulted in a mangled text because, once the situation in which it was originally confronted was gone, there was no way to face such things? Dionysus may be unapproachable outside the Athenian theater of Dionysus, and perhaps such spectacles *should not* be watched except in circumstances like those for which they were intended. The restored text has been brought to life in the theater. Modern technology broadcasts the Greek drama to our living rooms and flies us to Athens in attempts to reproduce the original context. But viewed alone at home, or watched in the company of strangers, the play must have an effect thoroughly different from the one it had in an Athenian festival two thousand years ago.

The *Bacchae,* like other Greek tragedies, is about looking together, among other things. While raising questions about Dionysus and the ordered, everyday life he disrupts, the play suggests further questions about the place of looking in civilized human life. How do human beings look at the world around them, at each other, and at themselves? Are there things that should never be looked upon, or should be viewed only in certain circumstances? Do rulers and ruled look differently when public policy is determined in different regimes? Is the looking of spectators in a theater related by nature to Dionysus; and is a festival like the one that once surrounded the play essential to the proper effect of such looking? Let us look together, first at Euripides' depiction of Dionysus in Thebes, and then at the festival that celebrated Dionysus in Athens.

Part One:
The Dionysian Tragedy at Thebes

i

Bacchus abolishes boundaries. This god shows up, oblivious to the lines and limits that define ordinary human life. "Having changed his form" (*morphên d'ameipsas,* 4) from divine to human, he is simultaneously god and beast, male and female, terrible and gentle. The geographical sweep of the Prologue depicts his disregard for natural and conventional distinctions alike. Transcending mountains, rivers, and great seas, he has moved over a huge diverse continent and made it one. Different races, languages, and even walled fortresses present no barriers. The coming resembles an itinerary for an army advancing from the east, but Dionysus's advent is an easy flow. The liquid sounds (*lipôn de Lydôn,* 13) indicate the ease with which he has come. Embraced by the already "mingled" (*migasin,* 18) Greeks and barbarians in Asia Minor, he returns to the "streams of Dirce and the waters of Ismenus." His sudden appearances are not through doors or gates or passageways. Liquid himself, he slips in.

For those touched by Dionysus, life ceases to be measured, articulated experience in place and time. The women who follow him are merely "Asians." "Having passed from" (*ameipsasa,* 66) their origins, they forget their former distinct lives in their single-minded devotion to Bromius. They exhort others to follow them, to be "displaced" (*ektopos,* 69). The stung Theban women resisted at first but, now, they too are "all mingled together" (*anamemeigmenai,* 37). They have left enclosed houses in a walled city to dwell on "unroofed" rocks on the open mountains. There the distinctions between human beings and the world around them are muted. The Bacchantes are not separated from the earth by walls, floors, and shoes. They've exchanged their shuttle sticks for thyrsus sticks, and now weave with ivy vines and living snakes. They are compared to birds, colts, and fawns; instead of woven cloth they wear animal skins. Their fire is not an instrument of art or domination. It is not used for cooking, forging tools, or warmth against the snows of Cithaeron. Nor does it harm them. Rather, it flows from their rods, like lightning, a visible charge from the god who electrifies them. They throw themselves to the earth and sweet liquids spring up—not in rivers, springs, or wells, but wherever the earth is touched. The god's bounty is so great that even storage containers are unnecessary. When Bacchantes dance, the whole mountain "bacchizes with" (*sunebakcheu'*, 726) them. But this mountain is not properly their place. They speak of Crete, and yearn for Cypris, Paphos, and Pieria, as well. Furthermore, their holy places are peculiar in that their sense of the holy precludes place as it is ordinarily experienced by human beings. As a proseletyzing cult, Bacchism aims at universality. The god could be anywhere, anywhere one is not confined by the constrictions and constructions of civilized life. He'll move on when he's done with Thebes. To worship Bacchus is to be in touch—with earth, air, fire, water—but not with any particular place. He promises a literal "no-place," "u-topia": no house, no city, no defined home on earth. The Theban counterparts of these uprooted women tear up trees by the roots.

The women who worship Bacchus "out of place" also live outside articulated human time. Neither natural nor conventional time punctuates their lives; they do not plan or wait. Unconcerned with time of year, they tend no crops or animals, and store no food or wine for the future. Their plants are ivy, bryony, and fir, evergreens whose looks do not reflect seasonal cycles, but whose lavish growth is a continual show of powerful life within. The ivy and vines grow freely, ungoverned by a set form that they must reach to be themselves. The Bacchantes live apart from men, mingling without regard to age, and their lives are unmarked by ceremonies of birth, growth, or death. The fertility god of seasons makes his followers barren. They leave their own infants and nurse young animals. New devotees must be made in the streets of the cities that generate them. The Bacchantes chant the remembered story of Bacchus, but they have no story of their own. They do not look back together upon their own pasts or forward to their own futures. Once again, being in touch makes them deeply out of touch as well. Immersed in the present, they are, at one moment, fast asleep on the ground and then fully awake and upright, or, at one moment, bloody from battle, and immediately after, clean and refreshed, with no memory even of recent experience. The ritual *orgia*—"works in service"—of this god require little time-consuming preparation. There are no embroidered robes, no burnt offerings, no altar or hearth, no statues, no organized feasts. In short, where there is no ordinary sense of time, there can be no articulated festival time; where there are no days, there are no holidays.

The Bacchic celebrants merge not only with the earth and other living things around them, but with the god himself. To revere Bacchus is to "bacchize" (*bakcheuô*) or to "bacchize oneself" (*katabakchioomai*). The verb does not take an accusative outside the subject. Instead of offering libations and food to a distant divinity, the followers of Dionysus drink him and eat him raw, ignoring even bodily boundaries to become one with him. Losing oneself in Dionysis is a reassertion of one's ties to the earth, but, at the same time, it is an attempt to assimilate oneself to the condition of the god. Dionysus needs no priest to mediate between himself and his followers, no prophet to explain him: "The leader—*exarchos*—is Bromius" (140) himself. Anyone at anytime can be in touch with the god.

Those who merge with the natural world and with Dionysus do so while merging with others. It's not surprising that the most willing followers of Dionysus are women, who are, perhaps, by nature most attached to and in touch with other human beings. To "bacchize" is to "thiasize the soul" (*thiaseuetai psychan*, 75). Like most Greek choruses, the women of the *thiasos*, the Bacchic band, speak in the singular: "I rush" (*thoazô*, 66) and "I shall hymn" (*hymnesô*, 72). But here the dramatic convention acquires special meaning as they are made one by their dress, slogans, and the dance. Individual heartbeats merge in the drumbeat, and ecstatic music moves them outside themselves, not to isolation, but to thorough communion. Even Cadmus and Tiresias feel it; they say they've forgotten they are old men. Feeling the same things, they slip into the dual (194) and share a line of iambic trimeter (189). They "clasp hands and together make a pair" (*xunapte kai xunôrizou chera*, 198); in Greek, they "join the horizon." "Counting out no one" (*diarithmôn d'ouden*) (209), the god "has made no distinctions" (*ou gar diêrêch'*) (206). As we soon see, the priest of Apollo and the founding father of Thebes never fully lose themselves in Dionysus.

But the maenads on the mountain are thoroughly merged. In a vase painting, Dionysus faces two women, but it is difficult to tell which of the four bare feet and arms belong to which. The *thiasos* distinguishes itself from hostile outsiders; left alone, it is a unit. The Messenger mentions three groups and the individuals around whom they gather, but the women don't attend much to the division. Within the *thiasos,* there is no opposition or competition, in deed or in speech. Once again, articulation is foreign to Dionysus. In contrast, the cattlebreeders and shepherds distinguish themselves from each other, as well as from an easy-talking city slicker, and from the mute domestic animals whom they again distinguish as young and mature heifers (737, 739). Like most messengers in the tragedies, the Messenger from Cithaeron has looked with others. He speaks in the first person *plural,* reporting that the herders argued about what they saw: they "matched common reports with each other in strife" (715). But the Theban maenads, like the Asian chorus, cried out "in one voice," literally, "with one mouth" (*athroô stomati,* 725). Later as they attacked Pentheus, "all gave voice at once" (*ên de pas' homou boê,* 1131). The homogeneous democracy of the Bacchantes merges into an impetuous "throng." *Ochlos* (117, 1058, 1130) is a word often used in political contexts to describe a fickle mob, female or male, as opposed to the *dêmos,* male citizens who assemble to discuss their own and the city's common business. Though the women sing antiphonal chants of some sort, there are no "winged" words among the Bacchantes. In Homer, the word *ameibô* is used for exchange between persons, exchange of speech or private possessions—like the self-conscious talk and trade between Diomedes and Glaucus in *Iliad* VI. In the *Bacchae,* it refers mostly to change of position or appearance. It signals not organized giving and receiving among separate individuals, but the fluidity of anything touched by Dionysus.

The communion of the *thiasos* precludes private as well as public relations. Ordinarily, human love begins in distinguishing the loved one from others. Later, lovers or friends rightly feel that they have become "one." Nevertheless, in love and friendship, the others like oneself also remain somehow other. The Bacchantes mention love— Eros or Aphrodite—only as symbols of peace and release. Since they make no distinctions within the communion, they do not recognize either permissible or desirable behavior in its separate members. Their gentle closeness is thus deficient love, just as their angry violence can only be primitive justice. Unlike friends, they look neither at nor with each other, and feel no profound admiration, pity, or fear for other human beings; they are too much in touch.

Finally, placeless, timeless, merging Bacchism is opposed to the human self-consciousness that develops from standing up and looking at the world, for Dionysus makes it very difficult to look. The maenads are characterized by constant motion, interrupted by falls to the earth. Euripides repeatedly calls our attention to the way in which the god confounds "up and down" (*anô te kai katô*)[1] turning the world topsy-turvy, and transforming the relation of vision to the other senses. In the Parodos, the women sing of their feet, hands, mouths, and hair. Those who feel themselves to have come alive through Dionysus evoke the *contact* senses: the feel of air, smell of smoke, taste of liquids, and sound of drums. In a later ode, they sing of the "pale-bare foot" dancing in the "green pleasures of a meadow" (863–67). The synaesthetic mingling of visual and tactile expresses wonderfully the powerful beauty of their undifferentiating awe. Similarly, when they sing of colors in the Parodos, the effect is kaleidoscopic. For them, color permeates and is diffuse; it does not define the contours or limits of things. They prefer night and shadows to light and clear lines. A vase painting depicts a dancing maenad with head thrown back and eyes open, but glazed over. Others shut their eyes. The dancer's freely moving body extends and crosses the defined vertical space he usually occupies.[2] Ordinarily, eyes see only when they are lifted on an upright body, away from the earth, and when they remain still long enough to gaze steadily. Through them, an autonomous individual takes in what is outside himself. But the Bacchantes "take in" the world in order to merge with it. By changing the relative status of the senses, Dionysus makes the world look different.

The *Bacchae* odes have been compared to Romantic nature poetry or to landscape painting. But the Bacchic attitude is very different from that of the poet who self-consciously looks at the natural world. This looking requires separation from, as well as kinship with, the ivy, snakes, fawns, and foals that twine, slither, and leap through a world with no horizon, a world in which they have not stood up. Wordsworth's poems, for example, are about mortality, time, memory, place, and his own changing perspective on nature and human life. He is a mature, self-conscious beholder who often looks with or addresses his observations to another. And he speculates about his kinship with and his distance from the world upon which he looks:

> For I have learned
> to look on nature, not as in the hour

Of thoughtless youth; but hearing oftentimes
The still sad music of humanity. (*Tintern Abbey*)

Immersed in the beauty of the land, the Bacchantes have never seen a landscape. The latter must be shaped by the seer—or painter—who frames the scene with boundaries and a horizon. When a Bacchic woman throws down the frame of her upright loom (*histos*, from *histêmi*, "to stand up"), she abandons all frames and the orientation that framing makes possible in human life.

One reason the *Bacchae* is so unsettling is that the Chorus, which in most Greek plays is tied to the city, here consists of unrelated foreigners; there is no community "point of view." Agave thinks she has seen and killed a lion (1175, 1238), and, with eyes rolling in her head, she calls upon her son to come look (1257). Instead of withdrawing in pity and fear, the women, for once, are eager to look: "I see and shall accept you as a fellow reveller" (1172). Their response to her invitation to eat expresses their revulsion, but they urge her to show her trophies to the citizens. The rest of the play is Theban business, and the Chorus hardly reacts to the dissolution of the city through which it has passed, but with which it has never looked. Agave finally comes to a standstill, away from her *thiasos*. Only then can Cadmus make her see that this is not a happy "spectacle" (*opsin*, 1232), that, indeed, it is "not the sort of thing to be seen" (*oud'hoion t'idein*, 1244). Dionysus affects human vision not only by preventing and distorting it, but by making those he touches unable to distinguish between what should and should not be beheld.

ii

Pentheus rejects the god. He speaks the language of opposition, not surprising in the grandson of Cadmus, who emerged from the barbarians to overcome a monstrous dragon, and reaped civilized Hellenes from these chthonic, even incestuous, beginnings. Pentheus has detached himself from these beginnings. *He* makes distinctions: between old gods and new, immortals and mortals, Greeks and foreigners, free men and slaves, men and women, Thebes and countryside, day and night, dignity and folly. He orders out the articulated divisions (781–83) of his male army against the female thyrsus bearers who mingle on the mountain. Pentheus trusts in gates and walls, jails and chains. Like his grandfather, he has a strong sense of his own. He must defend "my" mother, "our" women—the Greek does not require the possessive—against alien forces. He will not be touched: "Do not put your hands on me, do not wipe off folly on me" (343–44), he cries. When the two old men who have clasped hands urge him to recognize the leveling god, Pentheus draws the line. But although he is so different from the Bacchantes, he, too, is characterized by his disordered vision. In both his public and private behavior, he is unable to look with other human beings.

King Pentheus is alarmed for the safety of his city. Most monarchs are vigilant about erotic alliances within their regimes, for the private friendships of those who see alike may result in invisible conspiracies against a king. There are no such friendships in Thebes and, as we have seen, the *thiasos* is characterized by an undiscriminating, blind form of "friendship." Though the maenads are unlikely to oppose the ruler in any political way, the presence of a communion of citizens who no longer feel their primary tie to be the city does constitute a real threat to ordered political life. But King Pentheus deals with this threat tyranically. Without father, mother, or friends, he looks and acts alone. The maenads are too much in touch to look with others; Pentheus, like most tyrants, is too out of touch. His grandfather has abdicated to him, and there is no council of advisors. He alone will spy out and act against opposition. Even the feeble chorus of elders, which provides a sort of public perspective in some plays, is absent here. And anyone—even a professional seer—who offers another point of view is suppressed.

Pentheus's public behavior is tyrannical in another way. Most kings rule by their manifest presence, often through public ceremonies or processions in which the ruler exhibits himself to his subjects, or in which they are reviewed by him.[3] Even without planned ceremonial occasions, the well-being of the community requires the visible presence of its different elements. Ruler and subjects might not look together as equals, but each is a viewer recognized by the other. Pentheus rejects mutual viewing just as he rejects mutual council: only he is to be on view; the city will look to him for its well-being; opposition must be hidden away in dark dungeons. He scorns even to look upon those who disagree (252).

Not surprisingly, the vision of the friendless tyrant is defective. His view of the women is based on what he's heard. "I hear" (*kluô*) he begins a long, distorting description of their imagined behavior (216 ff.). He "knows" of Tmolus by "hearsay" (462), and mistakes a bull for the odd-looking stranger who makes him want to *hear* more about the maenads. The eyewitness report of the Messenger from Cithaeron, in the central scene of the central episode of the play, looks both back to Pentheus's hearsay envisionings and forward to his disastrous firsthand view of the Maenads. "Having seen the sacred Bacchantes" (664), he says that Pentheus, too, would have *seen* (737, 740) that the *thiasos* was a "wonder of good order to see" (693). "Having seen these things," Pentheus "would have come with prayers" (712–13). Then he describes the attack on the villagers. In a striking image, he reminds us of the way in which human eyes almost reflexively close to avoid seeing what should not be exposed to view: "the garments of [bulls'] flesh were drawn apart more quickly than you could close the lids over your royal eyes" (746–47). The Messenger continued to watch this Dionysian dismemberment. The "terror"(*deinon*), he says, was "a sight to see" (*heam'idein*, 760).

From now on, Pentheus's concern shifts from his public responsibility to his private needs. For, suppress him as he will, Pentheus, too, yearns for Dionysus. No longer satisfied with reports, he develops a great "desire" (*erôs*, 813) to see the maenads with his own eyes (811), to become a "watcher" (*theatês*, 829). He says he would be sorry to see them drunk, but Dionysus remarks that all the same, he would see these "bitter things" with pleasure (815). To look differently, Pentheus must look different. He dons the "costume" (*stolên*, 828) of a maenad but, unlike the women, he is painfully self-conscious. His posturing betrays the armour between himself and the "effeminate form" (*gynaikomorphê*, 855) he has assumed; it is both shared costume and protective disguise. He says he has been "playing the Bacchant" (*bakchiazô*, 931). The verb differs slightly from the one used by the Chorus (*bakcheuô*); it suggests the difference between engaging in one's own activity, and watching oneself assume the customs of others. Pentheus's carefully delineated world has begun to blur. Hallucinating, he sees two suns and a double Thebes. The stranger, who at first seemed "not unshapely" (*amorphos*, 453), now appears in other shapes. The transformed king is led off in a peculiar private "procession" (*pompê*) unacknowledged retainers who later report what happened, and by the stranger, "the leader of our viewing" (*theôria*, 1047).

Unlike the maenads who fall to the earth, Pentheus rises far above it, an isolated "spy" (*kataskopos*, 916, 156, 981) and a "spectator" (*theatês*, 829) of the absorbed women below. Once again, his looking is aberrant. Pentheus is a voyeur. In the private realm, he wishes not to do, but to view, everything. The sexual voyeur watches actions that, by nature, should not concern anyone but the actors. By ignoring the line between private and public, he obliterates both realms. Other voyeurs who stare unblinkingly at the corpses of the dead, or the grief of the living, also see what in civilized life must be obscene, off-stage. The voyeur may seek out spectacles of bestiality, incest, necrophilia, cannibalism, and other violations of the natural lines of human life. Pentheus surely is titillated by the suggestion of such things among the maenads. In collapsing the distinctions between private and public, seen and obscene, human and animal, the voyeur may appear to embrace Dionysus. But the embrace is false. Although the Bacchantes, like animals, do not properly look with others, they do look—in their fashion—in the presence of others. As we have seen, the voyeur lacks their unself-conscious innocence. His furtiveness reveals a deliberately violated sense of shame that they do not have; he knows he should not be looking. We call him "bestial," suggesting not nature, but degeneration.

The voyeur's vicarious embrace of Dionysus is false also because, although he is somehow moved by what he sees, he is an isolate, outside communal, as well as private, combinations. Pentheus wants to see "the things he should not see" (912), but *his* looking must be seen by no one; he must not be touched. Even as he ignores boundaries, he erects a frame around others like himself, reducing their actions and passions to material for his viewing. Pentheus's private spying, like his public violence, is tyrannical.[4] Earlier, he speaks only of the maenads' physical behavior; now, too, he can see only what their *bodies* are doing. He cannot share their spiritual joys or sorrows or "thiasize the soul" with others; at the end he feels only the "pain," or "grief" (*penthos*), of Pentheus. In a terrifying reversal, this solitary and too-distant onlooker is drawn swiftly into the scene. Seen by those who do not ordinarily look up, he is pulled down to the earth he denies in himself. Earlier he anticipates being held by his mother; now he reaches out to touch her cheek and is ripped apart, his ribs "laid bare" (*gymnounto*, 1134) like those of the animals the Messenger describes. The corpse, dismembered and unburied, will be displayed for all to see. The young man who would maintain distinctions is almost eaten, reabsorbed, by his own mother, in a terrifying violation of human time and relations. His city is shattered; its founder will be transformed into a snake and will lead a mingled barbarian horde against the Hellenes he once civilized. Exiled by Dionysus, he will return to "ravage the oracle of Loxias," that is, of Apollo (1336).

Apollo's priest had warned Pentheus to join him in recognizing the new god. But like the god he already serves, Tiresias remains somehow aloof, always looking from afar. His rationalized arguments on behalf of Dionysus seem alien to the spirit of the god of unmediated mergings. He is a Theban, yet he has the distance to look into Theban affairs and see more than those whose primary allegiance is to the city. Like the Bacchantes, he is in touch with a god; but he is somehow out of touch with other human beings; unmarried and childless, he has been male and female; he has looked upon copulating snakes, and once he beheld the goddess Athena naked, as she bathed. Unlike the followers of Dionysus, he transcends the city in isolation. His blindness, though related to his insight and foresight, precludes his looking together with others. He alone is not punished, but it is clear that Apollonian vision, as well as the looking of shameless Bacchantes and voyeur-king, is inadequate when Dionysus shows himself in Thebes.[5]

Part Two:
Tragedy and the City Dionysia at Athens

Imagine another city, one that tries to provide an entire community with something like the experience of those who lose themselves in Dionysus. We are all familiar with revels that sanction temporary release from daily life: medieval festivals of Misrule, Twelfth Night, Jewish Purim, Catholic Mardi Gras, and camp topsy-turvy days. These are characterized by reversals or blurring of political and sexual hierarchies and distinctions, by unusual masks and costumes or no clothing at all, by dramatic role-playing, by wild dancing, or by the conspicuous consumption of intoxicating beverages.

The most important of the Athenian festivals was called the City Dionysia. The name differentiates it from rural festivals by attaching it to the physical "city" (*astu*); the location is crucial. This festival was far more than ephemeral entertainment; it was an important part of the positive training of the Athenian people.[6] Let us delay considering the dramatic highpoint of the festival and speculate about how the arrangements that led up to it address the unsettling questions the *Bacchae* raises about Dionysus, looking, and the city. We shall also consider some modern counterparts.

Like other civic events, this annual festival is characterized by its attention to shared time and place. In late March, summer agriculture and war do not demand the full attention of the citizens. The seas are navigable again, and allies send ambassadors to bear tribute and also to look at the first city. In the spring, the citizens are constantly aware of the distinctions between themselves and outsiders, as well as between themselves and resident aliens and slaves within the city. As we shall see, the community that assembles to celebrate the god who obliterates boundaries is conspicuously divided into distinct groups throughout the festival.

As in most civic business in Athens, responsibility and preparations are shared. Though inefficient, this arrangement insures continual participation in public life. Like other projects whose parts are contributed piecemeal by private citizens who order and pay for them, the festival involves large numbers of people. Several months before, the Archon Eponymous, the second chief magistrate in Athens, and his aids, none of whom is required to have any special training in drama, choose the poets who will enter the competitions. Actors are assigned and a preliminary selection of judges is made from among the tribes. The ten names of these ordinary citizens[7]—not drama critics—are put into sealed urns in the Acropolis; tampering with them is a capital crime.

Also chosen long before the festival are the *chorêgoi,* private citizens from different tribes, each of whom is assigned a poet and actors. It is the responsibility of the *chorêgoi* to provide money to outfit and train dithyrambic and dramatic choruses and flute players. This duty is called a *leitourgia,* a work on behalf of the *leitos* (folk). Unlike the Bacchic *orgia,* the *leitourgia* is the civic duty of an individual, freely assumed, or assigned, by tribe or city. Other "liturgies" equip a warship or finance a delegation to a panhellenic festival. This great public giving allows an individual to exhibit his wealth, but to do so in partnership with the city, which pays the actors and endows poets' prizes. A liberal *chorêgos* spends gladly; though compulsory, the *leitourgia* is not a tax. His giving, like all noble action in a small homogeneous community, is meant to be seen. During the festival, the *chorêgos* exhibits not only his chorus, but himself, dressed in splendid robes, as a noble object for the contemplation of his fellow citizens. This office seems to speak to Rousseau's warning in *The Social Contract* against the substitution of money for public service. In fulfilling his civic responsibilities, the *chorêgos* offers, in Rousseau's terms, *both* his "pocketbook and his person";[8] he expends *himself.* Compare him with modern "philanthropists." The word suggests that the benefactors act for all people, and not just for those in their own city. They also act in their own way, often privately, and even anonymously, endowing museums, parks, and theaters of their own choosing. At another extreme, a manual for producers of community dramas warns against a single patron because even financial dependence on one person reduces the community or group effort.[9] The modern representative republic often seems either to put *all* the responsibility into private hands, or to fear private initiative. The ancient participatory democracy requires the wealthy citizen to spend his wealth honorably, and then displays him and his work as examples of civic liberality—even magnificence—befitting a free man among equals.[10]

The *Proagôn,* before the poets' contest (*agôn*), takes place one or two days before the festival. Here the public is officially given the details of the program. In the Odeum, a hall near the theater, each poet stands with his *chorêgos,* actors, flute players, and chorus, to announce the titles, and perhaps plot summaries, of the plays. The civic meaning of the *Proagôn* is clearer when compared with our practices. It is not a review by an outsider who discusses and perhaps recommends the play. Nor is it a coming attraction in which potential spectators are enticed by samples; there will be only one performance. Rather, it is an occasion for the many citizens who will be acting to display themselves in their own persons, as fellow citizens, to those who will be watching. In the *Proagôn,* no one wears masks or theatrical costumes.

The last event before the festival period is the torchlit night procession commemorating the coming of Dionysus to Athens. The god's image, removed earlier from the temple in the theater precinct, is carried back from the northwest Eleutherae road to the theater. The procession is the first properly "Dionysian" event but it differs strikingly from the various manifestations of the god in the *Bacchae.* Here again, we see how the City Dionysia links *orgia* with *leitourgia.* Instead of lightning appearances and the removal of the population to the mountain, here a man-made statue of the god is deliberately carried within city walls, through gates and streets, and placed in a building made for institutional worship. It is escorted by armed *ephêboi,* young men in training to defend the city, but who are not yet full members of it. Like the festival period, they are on the border between civic and noncivic time. In the *Republic,* Socrates would forbid them to watch plays and would restrict their spectacles to the noble warfare of their elders.[11] In his *Letter to D'Alembert,* Rousseau suggests that they attend community dances instead of the theater.[12] Athens requires the young men to be present at the theater festival, but carefully regulates their role.

The next day begins the period during which all ordinary business is suspended. There is no assembly during the festival, and no legal action may be taken. Jailed prisoners are released on bail. The first official event, a turbulent procession, the *pompê*, is not an occasion for careful looking and distinguishing. Pressed together, or even from the sidelines or a reviewing stand, one forms not a view of the whole, but a fragmented, kaleidoscopic impression. Though it is difficult to gaze steadily, one is intensely aware of moving bodies, arms, bellies, noses, backsides, and ritual phalluses.[13] Citizens and foreigners, old and young, men and women move to the same throbbing rhythm. Many wear masks, and perhaps costumes, which blend their identities with those of the opposite sex or the god they celebrate. The arrangements do, however, maintain some shape, some direction. Now the physical forms of the city, which may have blurred in the flickering torchlight the night before, are visible. The procession winds through the streets, halting in the agora, perhaps for choral dances at the altars of other gods. The *ephêboi*—young men about to become citizens—sacrifice a bull and present the choicest parts to prominent city officials. Unlike the mingled Bacchantes of all ages, only unmarried girls take part in the *pompê*. A maiden of noble birth leads, carrying a golden basket of offerings. Others bear wine, now mixed with water, and food, now cooked with fire, to be consumed on the way. The abundance of Dionysus in Athens is enclosed in pots, baskets, wineskins, and other man-made containers. The rich ride in chariots. Prepared costumes identify other groups: citizens in white, metics—resident aliens—in red, and *chorêgoi* in their finery. However immersed in the crowd they are, the celebrants enter the theater of Dionysus together, in public procession, as citizens of Athens. They are one, but the one is an articulated community, not a *thiasos*.

The *theatron*—watching place—where the entire city will spend the next few days, from dawn to dusk, is a round space, like both a natural dell and a conventional agora, or an enclosure within a city wall. Most of the spectators sit closely, knee to knee, with nothing between them. This seating increases the sense of community. Jean-Louis Barrault remarks on the warmth and unity of "houses" where there is only one armrest between seats:

> The spectator is part of the others . . . the audience is a sort of synthesis of the whole community of the world, of the promiscuity of all the others pressing one against the other; a sort of human stirring shoulder to shoulder . . . which releases . . . a monstrous god, a sole personality. . . . The audience is a kind of enormous baby . . . all the adults lose their personality.[14]

This might recall the Bacchantes. But it does not describe with sufficient subtlety the Athenian theater, or the way in which "the monstrous god" comes there. The congregation includes the free male citizens—the Assembly—who often gather in a similar amphitheater on a nearby hill; the festival gathering is not the first time they have formed a community. They are uniformly encouraged to attend— Pericles arranged for the city to provide tickets for all—but they are not mingled indiscriminately. And, while they are joined on this occasion by many resident aliens and foreign visitors, the aim is not a "synthesis of the . . . world." Rather, grown men, *ephêboi,* maybe women and children, metics, and visitors, sit in separate sections, identifiable in their colored robes. Citizens may sit by tribe. It is the city of Athens that is foremost, and not the unarticulated "world." It has been conjectured that the wooden bleachers, which were later replaced with stone ones, were made from the timbers of Persian ships that these men, or their fathers, defeated at Salamis a few years before.[15] Whatever the facts, it is important to remember the occasions on which they gathered together in the past.

Finally, there is another kind of seating—front row stone thrones for polis officials, generals, and *chorêgoi.* Unlike Bacchantes who sit close together and look at nothing, or Pentheus, who sits alone and spies on everything, these "distinguished" citizens sit together and apart, viewing and on view. Most prominent, at the center, sits the priest of Dionysus, city official and intermediary between the god and his celebrants. Gone is the *exarchos* who whips up the moblike *thiasos* to ecstatic identification with Dionysus. A statue of the god who always looked alone in Thebes, now joins Athens as a fellow spectator at his own festival.

Dionysus is present in his altar as well. The flame that burns in the orchestra throughout the festival is neither the useful fire with which humans master nature, nor the narthex fire that streams spontaneously from the wands of dancing Bacchantes. The altar fire is for *looking at,*[16] not by solitary individuals or private households, but by the whole city together.

The visual focus of the theater is the round dancing place (*orchêstra*) of the chorus and the platform (*skênê*) where the actors perform. This platform usually represents the outside of a palace. There is no drop curtain to separate audience from acting place. Unlike modern theatergoers who sit before an implied fourth wall, almost like voyeurs looking into a private place, Athenian spectators, like the dramatic characters, observe what is normally on view to the public.

But while attention is focused on the stage, it is not exclusively so. The performance takes place in the daytime, so the acting area is not a lit place in a dark space. Daylight preserves distinctions that break down in the dark. Changing as the day passes, it keeps those who concentrate on artificial stage time in touch with natural time. Since the theater is so large, the figures on stage are small, distant, and undetailed. The well-lit audience, which sits almost circularly around them, is thus as much to be seen as the performers on stage. Citizens in the theater of Dionysus are far more aware of themselves and their fellow spectators than are spectators of modern plays and especially movies, strangers who are absorbed by the illuminated action at one end of a dark, rectangular room. Television, which enables viewers to watch in common but in private, *all* the time, with no preparation or cooperation before the viewing, seems the complete antithesis of the civic viewing we are considering. The modern extended republic does its governing through representatives, now mostly seen at a distance, on television. It is not surprising that those who stay home to view Thanksgiving parades organized by private businesses will view anything else that is shown. Electronic inventions have the potential to turn millions of viewers into voyeurs, who see without being seen, and keep in touch only by looking from afar. This technology may produce extreme unity and homogeneity but, at the same time, extreme isolation. Such isolation was less possible in the Athenian arrangements for overseeing public policy and viewing dramatic performances in full view of one's fellow citizens.

What else would one see from the Athenian theater? The mountainous scenery in some film versions of Greek tragedies is beautiful, but tends to remind most of us that we are foreigners. The landscape beheld by the Athenians from the theater is their own; it surrounds the alien subject matter of the tragedies, grounding the spectators in the familiar, even as they are transported by the spectacles on the stage. The theater in Athens is located at the margins of the city, and the spectators look south, toward the sea. They are outdoors, in touch with the weather and the natural contour of the hill they sit on. But even as they face away from the city, they are still aware of the presence of man-made Athens above and behind them. The unsettling wonders they will behold in the plays are still, somehow, framed by the solid citizens and solid foundations of the city that makes the festival.

Before turning to performances, let us glance briefly at some of our contemporary American festivals. In the context of our present discussion, they have a decidedly uncivic look. Popular *theater* festivals sell tickets long distance, mostly to nonresidents, and import famous actors who perform for audiences that have never before assembled and never will again. They gather at various Stratfords, for example, to "see shows." Our diverse and tolerant republic is rich in the variety of local ethnic festivals that are celebrated traditionally, often with the help of quite different friends and neighbors. But, in America, these festivities cannot be *civic* festivities, and it is evident that in a prosperous, mobile, and cosmopolitan society such traditions tend to atrophy. National holidays like Thanksgiving, Independence Day, and presidents' birthdays do not seem to have the same intensity as local or ethnic celebrations. Another variety of contemporary festival self-consciously aims to bring together a diverse urban community. A recent Chicago-fest was run by a nonlocal business called "Festivals Incorporated." It offered food, crafts, entertainment, and publicity for the incumbent mayor, but deteriorated into racial wrangling. In Annapolis, Maryland, a national beer company sponsored for several years a "city" festival which was heavily attended by outsiders. It was advertised in the *Washington Post* among other area "Festivals, Festivals, and more Festivals" from which a private family might choose a spring outing. Most of the pleasant fairs and festivals in hundreds of American towns have a commercial basis; their most visible activity, amidst preparations, decorations, and entertainment, is the exchange of merchandise; the crafts displayed for looking are for sale, as is the food.

Our hunger for something that sounds like more than just a commercial fair has taken an interesting form in the past few years—food, crafts, and entertainment in a setting of medieval and Renaissance exotica. For example, at Columbia, Maryland (a "planned community" with a heterogeneous population that works in other cities), a corporation started in Minnesota began a Renaissance Festival to celebrate another place at another time. The *Washington Post* ad announced, "the sixteenth century is back by popular demand." The event proved so successful that it is now held at a permanent fairground, more conveniently located just outside Annapolis. Perhaps the sixteenth-century fair was also primarily a commercial enterprise. But this "holiday" festival of cosmopolitan modernity is very different from that of the ancient polis. Let us now return to the theater in Athens.

In the first watched performances, choruses from each tribe sing dithyrambic hymns, often about Dionysus. But unlike the identically masked, rootless Asian women in the *Bacchae,* these singers are native-born men and boys, the present and future citizens. They are released from their required military training to be trained for the festival. Their trainer, though not a poet, must also be native to the city. As worshippers of the god, they sing and dance, bound into a circle, crowned with flowers and ivy, but they are *unmasked*. Far from losing their identities, they remain distinguishable from each other and identifiable by their fellow citizens. Nor are the spectators moved outside themselves by these hymns, since the singers are not fictional personages with whom they identify.[17]

The next day begins with a political display in which the city exhibits itself for its own citizens and for outsiders. After the priest of Dionysus purifies the theater by sacrificing a pig and pouring libations, there are processions that, unlike the earlier parades, are entirely for watching. Young Athenians march before the vast assembly, carrying jars of silver talents, the year's tribute from allied cities. Citizens and strangers are honored for their services to Athens. The orphaned, but now-grown, sons of men who died in battle parade in full armour. They have been educated by the city, which now displays them as they make the transition from wardship, and seat themselves as fellow spectators, among the citizens.

Now at last is the gathered city prepared to look upon what is alien, alien not only because the dramas depict semidivine heroes, kings, and assertive women of other cities at other times, but because, in them, civilized people must confront anew what they have made alien to themselves: their own buried monstrousness. The great chorus in *Antigone* articulates a paradox about man: the very thing that makes this *anthrôpos* wonderful makes him terrible. To be *deinos* is to be tragic. Human beings are articulating beings who rise up and distinguish themselves from the world and from other beings in the world. Only humans are conscious of place, time, and mortality, and only humans distinguish between what they will do and look upon from what is forbidden. But tragedy reminds us that humans are also the only beings who essentially strive to ignore or overcome such limits. Like voyeurs' peep shows and everyone's dreams,[18] the tragedies reveal rape, parricide, incest, cannibalism, and defiled corpses; their subject is human *hubris,* the violation of limits and the failure to articulate. In the theater, spectators must face what is mixed and mingled, mangled and impure.

To understand the theater of Dionysus in Athens, one might have to understand why Oedipus ends his life in Athens. Repeatedly, the plays show us a tragic protagonist from Thebes—or someplace like it—who brings terrible and wonderful experiences to the most civilized city in Hellas. Athens is not simply providing a refuge for them. These extraordinary sufferers are somehow gifts: gifts to insure the fertile, vital humanity of the city that takes them in. Consider Thebes, the paradigm tragic city. Cadmus comes from the East, brings the alphabet, slays a dragon, and turns a violent, chthonic, incestuous settlement into a walled and orderly city. Then Dionysus is engendered there and, when he returns, the women run for the mountain. The young king is killed and the city is shattered. After a few generations, another watchful king exposes a baby on the mountain to avoid predicted disasters. The baby, who grows into a fully developed version of Pentheus, returns to subdue the raw-eating sphinx-monster that has attached itself to this city. Answering all questions and requests himself, standing above the earth and the city, taunting the gods, this autonomous paradigm of all human beings kills his father, sleeps with his mother, and generates his own siblings. Years later this untouchable—now blind and dependent—comes to Athens, to a sacred grove containing the threshold to the underworld. Adopted by the city whose ways he must now *feel* out, and recognizing the power of love, he now gives not his power to dominate or control, but himself. Theseus recognizes that to accept him is to worship earth and sky "at the same time" (*hama, Oed. Col.,* 1654). It is not clear whether Oedipus vanishes up or down or what he tells Theseus, but at last he leaves something that will pass down properly through generations of Athenians. Thebes, the city of violent beginnings and obscene reversions, of vines and wines, of dragons, snakes and sphinxes, of maimed walkers-on-earth, and of the wild mountain, has come home to Athens, the city of peaceful beginnings and visible progress, of the rooted olive tree, of skilled horsemen, and the tamed sea. Athens is deepened by this presence.[19]

The plays, then, are emissaries between the community and what it must usually exclude. Like Oedipus, the tragic drama is a necessary pollutant, "terrible to see, terrible to hear" (*deinos men horan, deinos de kluein, Oed.Col.,* 140–41). Like Oedipus, it is also a blessing to civilized human beings, to reconcile them with their primitive, yet ever-present, origins—with the buried dragon's teeth. But these *deina,* "terrible things," are now, in the *Bacchae,* "most terrible to men, yet most gentle" (*deinotatos anthrôpoisi d'êpiôtatos,* 861). On the mountain, Dionysus makes one forget the bitter things; in the theater, he recalls them, so that remembering and looking are sweeter than forgetting and turning away.

Athens understood that to be fully human, *deinos anthrôpos* must recognize both static, pure Apollo, and dancing, drunken Dionysus, and to come to "see" in the ways of both gods. Officially sanctioned Dionysian festivals, and the arrangement by which the Delphic shrine was given over to Dionysus for several months of each year,[20] both bear witness to this understanding. But like Tiresias's arguments, other festivals—even the sharing at Delphi—fail to recognize Dionysus fully. The difficulty is that they are all from the point of view of Apollo. One measures off part of the year, contains it within strict boundaries, and permits a weak version of once-powerful devotions. "Nothing in excess" (*mêden agan*); "measure is best" (*metron ariston*), we hear Apollo say, even as the revellers toss their heads and drink their wine. The wisdom that says one must know oneself and that both Apollo and Dionysus are that self is an Apollonian wisdom. One temporarily forgets oneself, under orders from the god of clarity, articulation, and the distant view. The difficulty lies in the *serial* character of these arrangements, the *alternation* of distance and participation, vision and touch. Pentheus's acting and looking are not Euripides' images of the theatrical experience. For true actors and spectators experience Dionysus and Apollo *simultaneously,* just as Theseus worshipped earth and sky, "at the same time."

The actor on the Athenian stage undoubtedly "identifies" with the alien character he impersonates. But behind his mask, he retains his self-conscious awareness of who he is. In the *Proagôn* he shows his own face; in the drama he shows the mask of Pentheus or Dionysus. The mask may call into question our fixed identities, may suggest Dionysian flux. But, we do not see one person transforming his very face into that of another.

The tragic Chorus is also simultaneously foreign and familiar. In the *Bacchae,* fifteen male citizens impersonate the Asian women. They sing of wild, timeless, placeless running, while executing dances that require the utmost attention to time, place, and direction. Though they speak as one and wear the same mask, they move in rectangular formations, always aware of rank. They sing of open spaces in the shadows and contact with the earth, but they dance in an enclosed space, in broad daylight, on a hardened orchestra floor. In complex diction and matched stanzas, they sing of experiences that obviate speech. They have committed to memory hymns to amnesia.

The spectators who behold the action on the stage are also *simultaneously* themselves and others. Only as separate, autonomous souls can they feel pity and fear for others like themselves, but clearly other. As democratic equals, citizens-friends, they look both at and with each other. And like friends who act for and see themselves in each other, they see themselves in those they watch on stage. Unlike the cave spectators in the *Republic,* they are not in the dark; they can turn their heads. They are aware, even as they feel the real joys and terrors of Dionysus, that they watch a framed imitation, a whole with carefully articulated parts. Looking *together,* they can face what, if experienced firsthand or seen privately, might destroy their humanity. The spectacle (*opsis*) contest, and actors, which Aristotle and some of his interpreters dismiss as unnecessary, allow for facing such things with others. Essential to the moral and civic ends of tragedy, they are the proper work of legislators, teachers, and citizens, as well as the costume maker.[21]

Let us pause again to consider some recent American theater experiments, of interest to us because they so often invoked Dioynsus, while differing radically from the theater that celebrated him in Athens. The "new" theater of the sixties took its cues from Cézanne and the cubists; it sought kaleidoscopic, collage effects unbound by frame or linear, articulated forms. Often looking to Eastern models, it was self-consciously "total," multimedia, not just visual. The followers of Artaud and his "theater of cruelty" agreed that Sophocles is too "fixed," that the theater must move away from looking, language, and "masterpieces."[22]

Athens brought Dionysus from the mountains through the streets, into the theater. Some "new" groups took their performances to the streets—to Times Square and Grand Central Station—in order to dissolve barriers between imitation and life. Others deliberately abandoned even the fourth wall convention and the distinction between watcher and watched, encouraging audiences to mingle with actors and to take part in the action. Distinctions between what is publicly or privately viewable lost their meaning in such spectacles; nakedness was a trademark of the new theater. The explicit goal was to create a democratic "communion" among all the participants, most of whom had never come together before. Paradoxically, this communion was to coexist with different reactions from different spectators. Everyone could do and feel his own thing, but together. Theoretically, any reaction was as good as any other in this "democratization of Dionysus,"[23] but the celebrants themselves have described violent conflicts.

The deliberate avoidance of hierarchy and rigidity was the goal of such groups as the Living Theater, the Orgy-Mystery Theater, the Any Place Theater, the Ontological-Hysterical Theater, and the James Joyce Liquid Memorial Theater! The name of Dionysus was often heard, even before the Performance Group produced its famous *Dionysus in 69*, in which actors, spectators, speeches, and sets maintained their fluid character from performance to performance. Having destroyed any distinction between actors and spectators, the performers sometimes had to protect themselves from overly enthusiastic participants in the pseudo-Dionysiac atmosphere they had created; Pentheus's agents removed them to a place of incarceration where they could still consider themselves part of the action.[24] The published text, in which the triumph of Dionysus is unequivocal, is based on Arrowsmith's translation of the *Bacchae*. It includes the ruminations of the director and members of "the Group," and close-up photographs of their writhing, bloodstained, naked bodies. It is, appropriately, not paginated![25]

The so-called "people's" theater thrived in the sixties during the most intense opposition to American "participation" in the war in Vietnam. But the "participatory" antiwar "happening" rarely explored broad questions of policy and conscience. It was often meant to substitute for, not to speculate about, political action. The Athenians participated in the decision to fight the Persians, and those who sat together in the Assembly fought together at Salamis. When they produced the *Persians*, however—and later plays as well—they remained spectators, and their judges *were* looking for universal masterpieces. What is the relation between ordinary action in Athens and festival and theatrical action during the Dionysia?

In their workaday world, the Athenians look together at the same things, from differing perspectives, in order to reconcile private interests in domestic policy. From a single shared perspective, they must also look together to formulate foreign policy for the whole city. This, too, is self-interest. Hindsight, present-sight, and foresight are for the sake of action. In their leisure time, in the theater, they feel and judge, but not from self-interest. These plays are also civic actions, but they are not for the sake of further political action. Like assembly, law courts, and war, the festival unifies the citizens. The plays at the heart of the festival also make them one, not from competing, but from *looking*, together. Just as festival competition is somehow higher than the competitive excellence of Athens at work, so also is play-watching superior to play production, because, in addition to prizes, glory, and

a beautiful product, it has *looking* as its end. Pythagoras said that
some people attend games in order to sell for gain, others to compete
for fame, but that the best come to see.[26] In the shared time of the
festival, and especially of the play, human beings cease trying to
control the world and others in it. They do not merely merge or
dissolve, but, for a time, they pause from working, building, and
fighting, to recall their relations to the earth, to other living things, to
each other, and to the gods. During the festival of Dionysus, looking
for the sake of looking is joined with dancing for the sake of the dance;
looking here means staying in touch. The thoughts that accompany
such looking are likely to transcend particular interests, and also
distinctions between people who belong to the city and others outside
it. Thus, to this assembly, Athens invites its resident aliens and
foreigners to behold both Athens and what Athens beholds. Many, no
doubt, are mere sightseers. But for some citizens and some strangers,
this dancing, looking, and feeling together may approach a communion
that far transcends that of the city and that of the Dionysian communi-
cants. Does this kind of looking require others—or very many others?
Do philosophic friends require civic festival times to direct their
attention to the things which transcend time? The few who emerge
from the cave in the *Republic* appear to be solitary spectators. Perhaps
they might read tragedies in private. But for most, at least, the
Athenian *theatron* is somewhere between the *thiasos* and *theôria*
(contemplation) and it aims at making them fuller human beings than
they would be without it.

Having made such high claims for the tragic highpoint of the City
Dionysia, I hesitate to bring us back to earth. But we must return, if
we are to be true to the spirit of the festival. Back to the *city* would be
more accurate, since, as we have seen, the earth and the city, though
in touch, are not to be confused. The exact order of the festival events
is disputed, but nearly all the schedules proposed agree that satyr
plays and comedies follow tragedies. Either at the end of each day, or
at the end of the festival, the spectators turn to different sorts of
Dionysiac representations. It is impossible to explore them fully here,
but we can at least note that both differ from tragedies in that they
depict unbounded appetites, distortions, and monstrosities as humorous supplements to regulated everyday life. They, like processions and
carnival merrymaking, can coexist with that life, without threatening
to shatter it. The comedy after the tragedy helps to *return* the partially
transported spectators to full citizenship, even as it mocks them.
Comedies were usually set in Athens. It became the convention in later

years for new arrivals from harbor and marketplace to come from the audience's right, the direction of the Athenian Piraeus and agora, and for arrivals from the open country to come from their left, the direction of the Athenian countryside.[27] Contemporary subjects, topical and personal allusions, and unmasked addresses to the audience as citizens, repeatedly break the dramatic illusion in comedies. The awarding of prizes, crowning of victors, and processions out of the theater, return them to ordinary time and place. The Assembly is the core of their nonfestival life and the appropriate setting for the formal transition back into that life.

The first business transacted by the Assembly on the day after the Great Dionysia is festival business. Now only the citizens gather in the theater to consider religious matters and complaints about the processions, contests, officials, and participants in the festival.[28] Such self-conscious emerging from festival to everyday time is strikingly missing from the mergings that are central to the Dionysian experiences we have examined in the *Bacchae*. And it rarely occurs after conventional theater and television shows—contained gaps in ordinary time—or after anti–establishment performances that deliberately blur the margins of the action. The conclusion of Mardi Gras in New Orleans provides a last example. A reporter writes that at midnight a bullhorn abrubtly announces that the holiday is over: " 'You must clear the streets for the street cleaners' . . . by morning the natives say, 'You'll never know it happened.' "[29] Mardi Gras takes over the city for a day; but like most of the festivals discussed above, it is not primarily a civic event. Exclusive "crewes" organize parades, crownings, and balls, and there is much general merrymaking, but the city does not gather as one.[30] Rather, it provides police protection and garbage disposal. The ends of the Great Dionysia and of the Mardi Gras are a telling contrast of ancient and modern notions of the ends of government.

In the *Bacchae*, the god says he will manifest himself "so that the city of Cadmus may see" (*horai*, 61). But Cadmus and his people somehow cannot "see" Dionysus and survive. The city of Athens arranges to look together upon Dionysus and those who have beheld him and, at the same time, to look upon those with whom they are beholding Dionysus. In this remarkable arrangement, it is possible, at least, that citizens may truly drink and dance, yet look and learn, and yet again return to their looms and to their Assembly on the day after.

We who live in a world where women no longer labor at looms, and free men may never set foot in assemblies, cannot return to the

Athenian polis. Nor would most of us want to, knowing that the coherent public life we have been examining was accompanied by rigid sexual distinctions, by extreme censorship, by slavery, poverty, and almost continual warfare. As we buy our machine-made clothing and elect our representatives, as we feast together after watching the parade in the comfortable privacy of our homes, as we choose our plays and movies, and even our festivals, we thank whatever god we will for our physical, political, religious, and intellectual freedom. But we, too, have paid a price, a price having something to do with Dionysus and with civic community. Perhaps we can avoid becoming intellectual voyeurs who restore the texts of unspeakable things, stage what should not be seen, and examine with unblinking curiosity the cares of a distant time and place, by keeping always one eye upon ourselves, and by asking what *our* souls and cities can learn from the ones at which we have been looking.

Notes

1. *Bacchae,* pp. 80, 96, 349, 552, 602, 741, 753.
2. See Erwin Straus, "Forms of Spatiality" in *Phenomenological Psychology* (New York, 1966), pp. 3–37. See also "The Upright Posture," pp. 137–65.
3. One might think of the progresses of the first Queen Elizabeth, or the coronation of her namesake. See David M. Bergeron, *English Civic Pageantry 1558–1642* (Columbia, S.C., 1972) and Edward Shils and Michael Young, "The Meaning of the Coronation," *Sociological Review,* 1, no. 2 (1953), pp. 63–81.
4. We might also remember Gyges, whose injustice and tyranny are related to his voyeurism. In the *Republic* (II), Gyges—or his ancestor—looks on an oversized, naked corpse in a hollow horse. The ring he steals from the body enables him to be present among people who cannot see him, and to do unjust acts with impunity. He soon commits adultery with the king's wife and takes over the rule. In Herodotus (I.8–13), the ruler of Lydia insists that Gyges look upon his naked wife. After this viewing, Gyges kills the husband and becomes ruler. Another solitary viewer of dead bodies in the *Republic* (VI) is Leontius. Although his anger and desire are at odds, it is not clear that intellect and desire are. Injustice and voyeurism are also related in the biblical story of the lustful elders who watch Susanna as she bathes. Their looking, as much a violation as their rape would have been, is related to their being corrupt judges, violators of community. Turning their eyes from heaven, they bear false witness, and are finally exposed because they could not properly look together with others.
5. I have found the following books most useful in thinking about the

Bacchae: G. S. Kirk's translation (Cambridge, 1979); E. R. Dodds's Text, Introduction, and Commentary (Oxford, 1960); R. P. Winnington-Ingram, *Euripides and Dionysus* (Cambridge, 1948); Walter F. Otto, *Dionysus: Myth and Cult* (Bloomington, Ind., 1965). Charles Segal's comprehensive study, *Dionysiac Poetics and Euripides' Bacchae* (Princeton, 1982), appeared as I was finishing this essay. I have eliminated some, but probably not all, of the overlapping material. Segal's book is indispensable for anyone interested in the *Bacchae* and Greek tragedy. I, too, have learned much from many of the authors he cites, especially René Girard and Arnold van Genneps. See also Marcel Detienne, *Dionysus at Large*, trans. Arthur Goldhammer (Cambridge, Mass., 1989), and *Masks of Dionysus*, ed. Thomas H. Carpenter and Christopher A. Faraone (Ithaca, N.Y., 1993), which also have appeared since this essay was first written.

6. I have found the following books most useful in thinking about the festival and about Athens: Alfred Zimmern, *The Greek Commonwealth* (Oxford, 1961); H. W. Parke, *Festivals of the Athenians* (Cornell, 1977); A. W. Pickard-Cambridge, *Dithyramb, Tragedy and Comedy* (Oxford, 1927). *The Dramatic Festivals of Athens* (Oxford, 1953). H. C. Baldry, *The Greek Tragic Theatre* (New York, 1971) is an easily available paperback introduction. *Nothing to Do with Dionysus: Athenian Drama and its Social Context*, ed. Froma I. Zeitlin and John J. Winkler (Princeton, 1990), which appeared after this essay was first written, contains a number of interesting articles about the political and social context of Greek tragedy. See especially Winkler, "The Ephebes' Song: *Tragoidia* and *Polis*"; Zeitlin, "Playing the Other: Theater, Theatricality, and the Feminine in Greek Drama"; Simon Goldhill, "The Great Dionysia and Civic Ideology"; and Ruth Padel, "Making Space Speak."

7. The generals were given this honor at some point. The point still holds; they were chosen because of their civic status, not on acount of artistic expertise. See Goldhill, pp. 101–2.

8. Jean-Jacques Rousseau, *On the Social Contract*, III, xv.

9. George McCalmon and Christian Moe, *Creating Historical Drama: A Guide for the Community and the Interested Individual* (Carbondale, Ill., 1965), p. 48.

10. Aristotle, *Ethics*, IV.

11. Plato, *Republic*, VI.

12. Jean-Jacques Rousseau, *Letter to M. D'Alembert on the Theatre*, IX.

13. Mikhail Bakhtin's *Rabelais and His World* (Cambridge, Mass., 1968) contains the best discussions I know of such periods of festival abandon.

14. Jean-Louis Barrault, "Best and Worst of Professions," in *The Uses of Drama*, ed. John Hodgson (London, 1972), p. 24.

15. E. O'Neill, Jr., "Note on Phrynichus' *Phoenissae* and Aeschylus' *Persae*," *Classical Philology* 37 (1942), pp. 425–27.

16. One is reminded of the Jewish injunction about Hanukkah candles: they are to have no utilitarian purpose, but to be only for looking. There is

conjecture that Hanukkah customs developed deliberately in response to rural Dionysiac rituals: Jews no longer need hide in the mountains like beasts, wild running is replaced by standing around an altar, inarticulate shouts by psalms of praise, and flowing torches by crafted candelabras. See Theodore H. Gaster, *Festivals of the Jewish Year* (New York, 1966), p. 252.

17. A thoughtful discussion of the civic status of the dithyramb can be found in William Mullen's *Choreia: Pindar and Dance* (Princeton, 1982). See also Winkler, "The Ephebes' Song" in *Nothing to Do with Dionysus*, pp. 20–62. Nietzsche's *Birth of Tragedy* consistently underemphasizes the institutional and civic context of both dithyramb and tragedy.

18. What does the *dreamer* behold? Often timeless, placeless, topsy-turvy, his dream is peopled with fluid personae who merge with each other and their surroundings. It may resemble the shifting life of the Bacchantes, who wake or sleep in an instant. Having no memories or restrictions when awake, perhaps they sleep without dreaming. The dreamer may experience what is unthinkable in waking life. Not only Jocasta has observed that, "in dreams many a man has lain with his own mother." Like a play, a dream is often *watched;* Homer's people "see" their dreams. The dreamer may be a spectator of his own actions; he may be the protagonist of the drama, or play all the characters. In such dreams, the line between watcher and actor is blurred or even disappears. Because a dream has no continuity of time or place with waking life, and no frame or context in which it is "seen," the dreamer is usually thoroughly absorbed by it. But, at the same time, a mysterious "second sight" says it is "*only* a dream." Dreamers who lose all awareness that they dream a contained imitation really choke, or scream, or wake, when the dream becomes too real, too "traumatic." They might remind us of theater spectators who miscarry when they see the Furies, who shoot the villain, or who run from the theater in fear. There is another sort of frame around the dream vision. Not prescribable, reportable, or censurable, the sweet dreams and hideous nightmares of civilized human beings are their own business. We cannot dream together, and so dreams can have ony the most indirect, unpredictable influence upon the waking life of citizens and city. Those legends in which men about to violate their motherlands dream of violating their mothers suggest that our dreams are not the realm in which to nurture viable community life. For examples, see Caesar in Plutarch and Hippias in Herodotus (VI.107). The waking tyrant *does* what other men would only *dream* of doing. The dreams of good people may be better than those of ordinary ones, but no one can learn to be good while asleep. Dreams, like voyeurism, offer a less disruptive form of Bacchism, but they are still private, in Greek, "idiotic," experiences.

19. I believe that a similar story is to be found in *Suppliants, Persians,* the *Oresteia, Philoctetes,* and Medea. Froma Zeitlin's interesting work on Thebes as a "commonplace" in Athenian drama has appeared since this essay was first published. See "Thebes: Theatre of Self and Society in Athenian Drama,"

in *Nothing to Do with Dionysus,* pp. 130–67, and "Staging Dionysus between Thebes and Athens," in *Masks of Dionysus,* pp. 147–82.

20. See H. W. Parke and D. E. W. Wermell, *The Delphic Oracle, Vol. I: The History* (Oxford, 1956), pp. 11–12, and Joseph Eddy Fontenrose, *The Delphic Oracle* (Berkeley, 1978), p. 207.

21. Aristotle, *Poetics,* VI.

22. Antonin Artaud, *The Theatre and Its Double* (New York, 1958).

23. Daniel Bell, "Sensibility in the 60's," *Commentary,* June, 1971, p. 73.

24. I am indebted to Gerald Weales for this information.

25. The Performance Group, *Dionysus in 69,* ed. Richard Schechner (New York, 1970).

26. Diogenes Laertius, *Life of Pythagoras.* The present discussion raises questions about the looking we do at sports events. Consider the funeral games in *Iliad* XXIII, their more civic counterpart in *Aeneid* V, the Panathenaea games in Athens, and the ancient Olympic games.

27. Baldry, p. 40.

28. The single most important source of information about the festival assembly is Demosthenes' speech *Against Meidias.* In 349 B.C., Demosthenes served as *chorgos* for his tribe's dithyrambs. Harrassed by Meidias before the festival, and publicly assaulted by him in the theater, Demosthenes won a preliminary motion against him in the theater assembly. The surviving speech was never delivered—an out-of-court settlement was reached—but it conveys vividly attitudes about the festival and its civic role.

29. *Washington Post,* February 25, 1982, B1.

30. In 1968 a group of newcomers to New Orleans, concerned about the aristocratic exclusivity of Mardi Gras, added an event in which everyone might participate. The new "Crewe," Bacchus, founded a night parade for the Sunday before the holiday. Sunday was chosen, in part, because it was prime television time. Floats were designed by a professional, and the event received nationwide coverage. The first king of Bacchus in this Catholic/civic festival was not a local citizen leader, but a famous Hollywood star, the Jewish Danny Kaye! See Myron Tassin, *Bacchus* (New Orleans, 1975). For the more traditional celebrations, see Duforn Huber, *If Ever I Cease to Love* (New Orleans, 1970).

The Comic Remedy in Private Spectacle

Machiavelli's *Mandragola*

In October 1525, Niccolò Machiavelli wrote to his friend Francesco Guicciardini to explain some difficult passages in the *Mandragola*—passages that had brought Guicciardini great "distress of mind."[1] In this letter, Machiavelli playfully clarifies a colloquial expression by commenting on a mysterious sonnet by a modern writer, Burchiello. Machiavelli says he believes that a person who considers the sonnet well "may continue to stir up our times."[2] He also refers to an ancient authority—"as Titus Livius says in his second decade"[3]—although he is aware that the second decade of Livy's Roman history is not extant. Perhaps his parody of a scholarly analysis of the "light material" (Prologue) of *Mandragola* should caution those who wish to read the play seriously as well as lightly: one must never forget that it is a staged comedy, "a thing to break one's jaws with laughter" (Prologue).

But since Machiavelli has the distinction of being both a playwright and an outstanding thinker apart from his plays, seriously amused readers should ask why this political theorist would repeatedly turn his attention to the comic theater. What is the relationship between his comic masterpiece and his revolutionary political treatises? The letter to Guicciardini, which seems to mock scholarly commentary, should stand as a check against the distortions of scholarship. Nevertheless, it should not discourage exploration of the sources, subject, and intent of Machiavelli's most famous and most original play. Indeed, the letter may even direct our attention to some of the central meanings of *Mandragola*.

Part 1 of this chapter will examine Machiavellian *virtù* in the light
of ancient virtue and of Christian virtue, through a discussion of
Machiavelli's attitude toward chastity. Central to this discussion is
Machiavelli's use of Livy in this play, as well as in the *Discourses*, in
a new version of the rape of Lucretia. Part 2 will examine, partly in
the light of Paul's epistles to Timothy, Machiavelli's view of Christian
man, in his depiction of the friar Timoteo and his flock. Part 3 will
make some suggestions about the relationship between morality and
the comic theater. But first, Machiavelli's Prologue to *Mandragola*
invites a prologue.

Prologue

The first stanza of the Prologue to *Mandragola* expresses hope that
the audience will "come to understand a new case born in this city"
(*noi voglian che s'intenda/un nuovo caso in questa terra nato*). The
aim of this essay is, in part, to come to an understanding of what this
means. In the comedy, as well as in the political writings, the claim to
newness must always be understood in relation to something old. A
reading of *Mandragola* should aim to clarify Machiavelli's attitudes
toward old things: conventional morality, the conventions of drama,
and the conventional purposes of drama.

Italian theater at the time Machiavelli wrote was dominated by the
influence of the Roman comic playwrights Terence and Plautus, who
modeled their plays on Greek New Comedy. In cities throughout Italy,
much time and money were devoted to research and productions, in
Latin or in newly prepared translations, of the Roman plays. Machiavelli's letters are peppered with allusions to them, and, like many of
his acquaintances, he translated one of these plays (Terence's *Andria*).
In addition to the revivals of Plautus and Terence, the end of the
fifteenth and start of the sixteenth centuries saw the growth of a new
native genre, the *Commedia Erudita*, based on the old Roman plots
and characters, but self-consciously refusing to be servile to antiquity,
and emphasizing such new elements as Italian settings, some indige-
nous characters, and a modern vernacular language.[4] The prologue
to Machiavelli's *Clizia* acknowledges its source as Roman comedy
(Plautus's *Casina*) and implies what Machiavelli's political writings
explicitly say: one can benefit from accounts of ancient times because
human nature does not change.

Mandragola begins with a conventional address to the audience, one that combines the techniques of both Plautus and Terence. It introduces what appears to be a new play in the style of the *Commedia Erudita*. The argument draws attention to the conventional street setting, and to the houses of familiar Roman characters—the young lover, the chaste maiden he loves, a foolish old man—and to one familiar modern one, the priest. The heroine's mother bears a name found frequently in the plays of Terence. Early in the play, Machiavelli jokes about his stagey exposition. Later, there are explicit, albeit humorous, references to unity of time, an ancient stage convention that Italian critics came to emphasize in the latter half of the century. The action of the play is more unified in the Roman manner than that in most contemporary plays. Thus, here, as well as in *Andria* and *Clizia*, Machiavelli indicates his familiarity with the ancient comic models. But unlike the plots of *Andria* and *Clizia*, the plot of *Mandragola* is original. While it might at first resemble new versions of ancient comedy and another popular new form, the novella of Boccaccio and Cinthio, Machiavelli's "new case born in this city" will prove to be newer in a more serious way than these already conventional novelties.

The fifth and sixth stanzas of the prologue continue to juxtapose old and new things. After the conventional Plautian presentation of the argument, the author begins, more in the defensive and threatening tone of a Terence prologue, to justify the "light material" of this work: no one appreciates and rewards his graver endeavors; this scorn for worthy actions is proof that "in all things, the present age has fallen off from ancient worth" (*l'antica virtù*). Readers of *The Prince* and *Discourses* will recognize a familiar theme from the introductory letters and prologues, and from passages dealing with the significance of the works and the importance of renovating and being reborn.[5] Machiavelli's repeated claim is that he will teach his readers new things by presenting them with ancient as well as recent ones. Again and again he urges the imitation of antiquity,[6] though, as we shall see, he often presents new versions of these examples for his own purposes. Machiavelli is fully aware of the danger of advocating the rejection of present practices and beliefs for older ones, and of revising old beliefs in order to set forth new ones. Thus, he says at the beginning of the *Discourses* that "it has always been no less dangerous to find new modes and orders than it has been to look for unknown seas and lands" (*D.*, I., intro.).[7]

Might the danger of presenting a "new case" explain why the Prologue to *Mandragola* is so reticent about claiming a didactic purpose, one that might even make its author seem as "wise and grave" as he says he wishes to appear? His contemporaries seem to have discussed widely the Ciceronian injunction that comedy should instruct, as well as entertain, the audience. Donatus's commentaries on Terence, recovered in 1433, repeated this precept and, though it was disregarded and even mocked in many contemporary plays, Machiavelli himself seems to have thought about it. In *Clizia*, less original in plot than *Mandragola,* and perhaps less novel in thought as well, the prologue speaks of the play's effect on youth:

> Comedies exist to help and to delight the spectators. It is truly very helpful to any man, and especially to young men, to recognize an old man's avarice, a lover's furor, a servant's tricks, a parasite's gluttony, a poor man's misery, a rich man's ambition, a prostitute's flatteries, the little faith of all men.[8]

However un-Ciceronian the lesson of *la poca fede di tutti li uomini* may be,[9] there is in *Clizia,* some explicit claim to teach. Similarly, in his "Discourse about Our Language," Machiavelli says that, although the aim of a comedy is:

> to hold up a mirror to private life, nevertheless, its way of doing it is with a certain urbanity and with terms which incite laughter, so that the men who run to that great delight taste afterwards the useful example that is underneath.[10]

Again, the meaning of "useful" is unclear, but at least the claim is made. One wonders why it is so muted in *Mandragola.*

Perhaps Machiavelli's reticence about this subject is due to his awareness that the lessons to be drawn from the "new case born in this city" are much more radically new than are those of a new version of a new version of New Comedy—that they differ greatly from the usual poetic attempts of older men to shape the young. If this were so, Machiavelli's comic drama about the "remedy" *Mandragola* would be as subversive of contemporary beliefs as the drastic "remedies" he discusses in the serious political works. To understand the relationship between these comic and serious remedies, we must see how Machiavelli rejects the older teachings—both ancient (Greek and Roman) and contemporary (Christian)—by presenting his dramatic new case.

Part One:
The Rape of Lucretia

Virtù: Public and Private

In form, *Mandragola* resembles ancient Roman comedy. But its plot is to be found in ancient Roman history, the very history Machiavelli claims as his subject in *Discourses on the First Ten Books of Titus Livius* and that he jokingly connects with *Mandragola* in the letter to Guicciardini quoted above. To understand what is new and what is old in Machiavelli's play and what he intends to teach, we must compare Livy's account of the rape of the Roman Lucretia and the events that followed with Machiavelli's account of the possession of a Christian Lucrezia and the probable results.[11]

Let us begin with the husbands. Livy depicts Collatine and his friends as warriors in the "vigor of youth,"[12] and their bragging and wager are described as a "boyish prank of the night."[13] These are the men who are soon to rise and overthrow the tyrannical Tarquins, and to establish a republican regime in Rome. The husband in Machiavelli's play, Messer Nicia Calfucci, is an elderly and impotent bourgeois lawyer who is ruled by women and can weep tender tears. His earthy Tuscan speech and his occasional regret that he didn't marry a country girl remind us that he is less sophisticated than the cosmopolitan city-slickers who trick him. Like most loyal citizens, he grumbles about his position in the city, but he is totally attached to Florence—by habit, by his timidity, and by his possessions. He is reluctant to leave, even for a short trip to the baths. He brags about his experience; but his foolishness, his lack of spirit (*animo*), and his professional concentration on books, render him unfamiliar with the "things of the world" (cose del *mondo*, III.2). The Prologue tells us he read much, especially in "Buezio." Machiavelli's strange spelling of Boethius might suggest that Nicia's decency is the sort of bovine mildness that is easily led by the nose. His name ironically suggests that he will be a loser. This essay will suggest that Machiavelli attributes the defeat of Nicia to the nature of his religion, to superstition, and to piety.[14]

Machiavelli's revised version of the man who would displace Lucretia's husband is more complex. In *Mandragola*, the hereditary tyrant of Rome is replaced by Callimaco Guadagni, whose ancient Greek and modern Italian names indicate his noble struggle for gain(s). The first song[15] seems to associate Callimaco with the unpolitical life. Like the nymphs and shepherds, he has lived for pleasure and comforts. An expatriate since his childhood, he has enjoyed a peaceful private life in Paris while the French king was ravishing his native country. Even in France, as he reminds his servant, Callimaco was unattached to any party or special interests, to any class, or even to any one pastime. When he decided to return home, he easily parted with all his goods. The arguments in which the would-be lovers first hear of the women they desire are also strikingly different. In Livy, strong warrior compatriots sit drinking around a campfire and argue about the virtue and honor of women. In Machiavelli, the "noble warrior" fled from war and heard of Lucrezia, the relative of an acquaintance, at a leisurely international gathering.

Sextus Tarquin returns to Rome alone and steals into Lucretia's home. He threatens to kill and defame her if she doesn't yield, and then rapes her. Lucretia submits in order to live and denounce her assailant, and then kills herself. In *The Prince*, Machiavelli argues that fraud is preferable to force in achieving the Prince's aims (*P.*, XVIII). Later, he asserts that the man of ability controls Fortune as if "she" were a woman (*P.*, XXV): she must be beaten until she is submissive to the strong man's will. In *Mandragola*, even a woman is best won not by force, but by fraud. In the new version of the siege of Lucretia, nothing is accomplished by coercion. As Nicia says, his faith in his deceiver is stronger than that of the Hungarians in their swords (II.2). His own little sword is only a comic prop[16] and he is swiftly conquered by a bold and risky plot in which the lover wins the cooperation of the husband and his mother-in-law, and finally, of the woman he desires. In place of the death of the dishonored Lucretia and the subsequent banishment and death of her violator, Machiavelli shows the continued life and honor of Lucrezia and her lover, and promises another life as the fruit of their liaison. Instead of the overthrow of a tyranny and its replacement by a republic, we see a thoroughly private man secure the pleasures that even a successful tyrant must usually forgo. Machiavelli's Florence is unaware of and unshaken by the acquisition of a new domain by the usurper, Callimaco Guadagni. Both lust and tyranny desire without limit, but, as Machiavelli suggests elsewhere, the private man can better afford to risk satisfying unlimited sexual desires. In this respect, the "regime" of the potent lover is less limited than that of the greatest potentate. The man in whom love plays the tyrant is the most tyrannical man. We must further explore Callimaco's relation to Machiavelli's great princes.

Although Callimaco is energetic and intelligent, he is unable to achieve by himself what he wants. As a result of his desperate passion, he is moody, frenzied, and even foolish. At one point, he contemplates suicide as an alternative to risky plots. His reason is dedicated to serving an irresistible desire that sometimes reduces him to confusion. This confusion is uncharacteristic of Machiavelli's greatest rulers. Callimaco is perhaps more like those second-level intelligences in *The Prince* who can discern and make use of what others understand (*P.*, XXV). Thus, he acquires an advisor who exercises *virtù* analogous to that exhibited by the most outstanding men. It is Ligurio (the "gloater" or the "tyer-up") who pulls the strings of the intrigue. He calls himself *capitano* and arranges his "army" (IV.9) to carry out this conspiracy. When Callimaco's *animo* fails, it is Ligurio who always thinks of a "remedy." Machiavelli plays down the gluttony of the Roman and Italian parasites on whom Ligurio is superficially modeled,[17] and emphasizes his sheer delight in imposing his will on others: "Your blood is in accord with mine and I desire for you to satisfy this desire of yours almost as much as you do yourself" (I.3). Machiavelli never allows him a soliloquy. This enhances his independence and authority, while depriving his companions and the audience of any clear knowledge of his motives. He feels a vague kinship with Callimaco, but *his* desire clearly has nothing to do with sex. As a former marriage broker, he knows the natures of men and women. Playing on the beliefs and desires of greedy, gullible, and fearful people, he plots with prudence, courage, and secrecy. He acts swiftly, spending the money of others, and, in Lucrezia's case, changes the nature of the conquered in order to secure his aims. By the end of the play, he has won not only the previously denied privilege of dining with Nicia but also the keys to his house. If Callimaco is the new "ruler" in that house, Ligurio has ruled the ruler. Thus, he is closely akin to another advisor of princes, Machiavelli himself.

Like the projects of Machiavelli's able princes and unlike Tarquin's, Callimaco's plot succeeds because the conspirators provide that their "good" or "advantage" (*bene*) benefits others. Thus, the remedy for Callimaco's unbearable discomfort coincides with the remedy for Nicia's and Lucrezia's childlessness. Nicia is not so simply a loser as his name might at first suggest. The same remedy relieves the pecuniary difficulties of Frate Timoteo and Ligurio. The remedy, of course, is not the medicinal *Mandragola*, but, as the song after Act Three says, "The trick [*inganno*] Oh remedy high and rare."

At first, Callimaco, like many tyrants, cares only for pleasure and the satisfaction of present selfish desires. But, like Machiavelli's prudent princes, and unlike ordinary tyrants—a word never used in *The*

Prince—Callimaco exercises restraint and thinks ahead. Although he doesn't hesitate to take another man's wife, he is not a conventional Don Juan. He is an adulterer but not a libertine. Unlike the Don, Callimaco proves his superiority by secretly succeeding in his conquest, not by flaunting a series of violations and, thus, courting his own fall. He will remain an undercover captain for as long as is necessary. But before the play is over, Callimaco has promised to be the godfather of his natural child and to marry that child's mother when her husband dies. The marriage proposal is his own addition to Ligurio's plan. The conquest, which must be enjoyed secretly at first, finally will be legitimate and Callimaco publicly will acknowledge himself the master of Messer Nicia's household.

Although Callimaco plans for the continuing satisfaction of his present desires, his success is limited by the limits of the field of action he has chosen. He himself recognizes the temporary character of his success:

> and if this happiness couldn't fail either through death or through time, I would be more blessed than the blessed, more saintly than the saints (V.4).

Though he can manipulate men and women and even Fortune, he cannot conquer death or time. This, above all, distinguishes Callimaco from the new princes whom Machiavelli discusses elsewhere. The language of love in Machiavelli's plays is derived from the language of war, and love itself is a battle to prevail.[18] But, because the conspirators invest all their talents and spirit in an undercover struggle for acquisition, there is no immortal glory for the victors. In Machiavelli's political works, the greatest prince eventually organizes everything anew in order to insure that the regime he founds will outlive him. The *Discourses* indicates that this is most possible in a glorious and long-lived republic. Love can only be a second-best activity for men like Callimaco (and Ligurio) who have forsworn politics. Where the end is a woman, there can be only an approximation of the struggles and successes of noble captains of men. Marital affairs are only a pale parody of martial ones.

Although Callimaco cannot be simply equated with the political men of *virtù* whom Machiavelli describes in other works, his new case does clarify some of the most difficult questions raised by those books. First, the play vividly presents individuals who embody the view of human nature on which Machiavelli's political teaching is based. Even though this presentation of human nature seems less harsh than the general statements in *The Prince*, the low desires of Timoteo, Nicia, Sostrata, and the anonymous Donna are the same as those of the subjects the prince might rule. According to a notorious remark of Machiavelli, men forget more quickly the death of their fathers than the loss of what they inherit from their fathers (*P.*, XVII). The play clearly indicates that Nicia's tender anticipation of fatherhood grows out of his concern for his estate: he wants an heir. Nicia and all of Machiavelli's people are characterized by an overriding concern for themselves. The play demonstrates this structurally. Many scenes begin or end with one of the conspirators spying on or doubting the loyalty of one of his fellows.

Concern for oneself seems to increase with *virtù*. The most striking thing about Callimaco is his detachment. Having lost his father as a child, and having no attachment to his fatherland, he is willing to father a child whose true connection to him will never be revealed. In addition to lacking country, parents, and brothers, Callimaco is a man without friends. In this he differs from the young lovers in the Roman plays. Ligurio is a recent acquaintance and an inferior. The former Paris companions are never mentioned in connection with Callimaco after the first scene. The goal for which Callimaco temporarily unites with others aptly indicates Machiavelli's view of human existence as an isolated struggle to prevail: success in the winning of a woman is unshareable. Love is often thought to be ennobling because it makes the lover less self-regarding. But sexual fulfillment for Callimaco is not characterized by affectionate union for the partner. Although he is called a "lover," and although the song after Act Two speaks conventionally of "loving another more than oneself," Callimaco's love for Lucrezia, like hers for him, is severely limited. They share their victory over a third party. She is attracted by his ingenuity and virility, which so contrast with the frustrating incapacity of her husband. He is attracted by the challenge of her resistance. In his plotting and in his success, his attention is always fixed upon himself. *Mandragola* presents the people among whom one lives primarily as the means and objects of one's desires. Love, friendship, and family affection are all contracted into self-interest.

The dominating principle of self-interest is seen even more starkly in the comedy than in the works with public subjects. In the latter, the common good of patriotism sometimes seems to mitigate Machiavelli's harsh view of selfish human nature and his advocacy of the extreme self-assertion of the prince. If Machiavelli plays down the force of

fatherly feelings and filial affections, he certainly advocates the exalta-
tion of the fatherland. The higher "common" good of patriotism thus
seems to justify the harsh and questionable means said to be necessary
for political ends. In the political writings, Machiavelli does not deny
the distinction between good and evil acts. Rather, he emphasizes
the need to weigh alternatives and make choices. *Mandragola* also
articulates this utilitarian principle, but the play's effect is to collapse
the distinction. Conventionally evil behavior is presented as good.[19]
The principles of *The Prince* are equally successful in high public and
in low private affairs. Machiavelli goes out of his way to emphasize
that the protagonist of his play is an *unpatriotic* man. The common
good of the play is nothing more than the sum of the private goods and
desires of the conspiring individuals. Finally, in the political realm, the
true and lasting success of the leader(s) requires that they improve the
subjects whose desires they must satisfy. Callimaco and Ligurio show
no such concern.

Virtue: Public and Private

Let us now examine more closely Machiavelli's attitude toward the
traditional virtue whose value is obscured in the course of the play.
Machiavelli's treatment of sexual transgression and its corresponding
opposite, chastity, can be taken as a measure of his attitude toward
vice and virtue in general.[20] An examination of relevant passages in
the political works will show how the play also rejects traditional
ancient (Aristotelian and Roman) and Christian notions of moral
virtue.

In *The Prince* and in the *Discourses*, Machiavelli warns against
violating the honor of the wives and daughters of one's subjects.[21] He
approves of Scipio's behavior in Spain, where he returned a daughter
to her father, and a young wife to her husband (*D.*, III, 20). Machiavelli
says that Scipio imitated the "chastity, affability, humanity, liberality"
of Xenophon's Cyrus (*P.*, XIV). But one can see from the references
to Scipio that a leader's concern with the virtue of women is merely
political, a means by which the *virtù* of men can prevail. Scipio's
"chastity" is an example of the calculated exhibition of a moral virtue
that the people wish to see in great men. The people are so attached to
such virtues that Scipio's return of the women, the most jealously
guarded of men's possessions, was more effective than force would
have been. Thus, as the conversationalists in Castiglione's *The Book
of the Courtier* agree, Scipio's "continence" was only a kind of

"military stratagem."[22] For Machiavelli, as for Cyrus, chastity is not valued for its own sake. *The Prince* makes clear that it is the *appearance* of virtue that insures support for a leader. Furthermore, Machiavelli even argues openly elsewhere that Scipio's "virtues" were not always as effective as Hannibal's "rapine" (*D.*, III.21).

These remarks about Scipio should be kept in mind when evaluating Machiavelli's strange unique reference to Aristotle as the authority for the view that "among the first causes of the ruins of tyrants [is] their having injured others with respect to their women, either by raping them or by violating them or by breaking marriages." (*D.*, III.26).[23] At this point he attributes the falls of Tarquin and the Decemvir Appius Claudius to their misconduct in this respect. However, other passages about Tarquin and Appius, whose experiences are closer than Scipio's or Hannibal's to the one dramatized in *Mandragola*, comment differently on the falls of these unchaste men.

Machiavelli discusses the fall of Appius Claudius, but he minimizes the outrage of his attempts to violate Virginia. Livy parallels the expulsions of the Tarquins and the Decemvirs and deals with the Virginia episode at great length. He reports the moral indignation of Virginia's friends and betrothed, and describes Appius's "crime" and "lust" and his attraction, like that of Tarquin for Lucretia, to the girl's modesty and beauty.[24] The Roman historian seems to agree with Virginia's father that chaste death is preferable to sullied life. The Roman people believe that Appius's ruin is due, in part, to the anger of the gods. In contrast, Machiavelli mentions Virginia only in passing, as another cause of disturbances when the insatiable Appius attempted to exercise his tyranny. Appius's greater, though perhaps related, defect was one of military stratagem: "being cruel and rough in commanding, he was badly obeyed by his troops" (*D.*, III.19). There is no suggestion of divine punishment for tyrannical lust.

Machiavelli tacitly comments on Livy's version of Lucretia both in his play and in his account of the episode in the *Discourses*. In the latter, he omits all of the passionate outrage found in Livy, and also present in Ovid's account and in Boccaccio's *De Claris Mulieribus*. There is no anger about the violation of a grave Roman matron's honor. Contrary to Machiavelli's later statement, the rape of Lucretia was not even the major cause of the fall of the Roman tyrant. It simply provided the first occasion for Romans to react

decisively to continued deprivation of their liberties: Tarquin was not driven from Rome because his son Sextus had raped Lucretia, but

because he had broken the laws of the kingdom and governed it tyranni-
cally. (*D.,* III.5)

In shifting the emphasis, Machiavelli says seriously in the political
treatise what the play depicts comically: chastity, like the other moral
virtues, is a matter of political prudence to be judged according to
the situation.

Machiavelli's teachings thus differ greatly from those of the authority he cites on the subject of women. Whatever Aristotle's conclusions
may be about the ultimate status of moral virtue, his rhetoric is
conservative of such virtue. The passage to which Machiavelli refers
is found in book 5 of the *Politics*, in the discussion of how the various
regimes can preserve themselves. Aristotle's advice to tyrants—much
of which Machiavelli transmits to his own prince—is stated in such a
way as to make tyranny less bad, to move it toward the more virtuous
monarchical regime. Perhaps his warnings against violating the women
of subjects should be read in conjunction with an earlier passage from
the *Ethics*. In his earliest definition of virtue as a mean, he emphatically states the opinion that some actions and passions do not admit of
means, that they are bad in themselves:

> nor is [acting] well or not well about such things a matter of [for example]
> with whom, and when, and how one commits adultery, but simply doing
> any of these whatever is to go astray.[25]

Although he repeatedly cautions against absolute rules in moral and
political matters, he does seem to approve of the opinion that there are
some deeds that are base, even if justifiable in extreme circumstances.
He discusses such circumstances with great delicacy.

Machiavelli's writings openly teach the use of virtue and vice in
clever alternation; no deed is ruled out. His play celebrates adultery,
and the *Discourses* approve of worse crimes in some circumstances.
The founding of Rome, made possible by fratricide, also required the
rapes of Rhea and the Sabine women. Machiavelli does not mention
these rapes but one can assume he could justify them if necessary.
Interestingly, Callimaco's description of his talk with Lucrezia sounds
something like Livy's Romulus wooing the Sabines after they have
been taken by force.[26] Callimaco's tricky seduction is, of course, a
more efficient way to get and keep *one* woman.

It is interesting that Machiavelli does not mention the famous adultery of King David, whom he holds up for imitation in the political

books.[27] For David, as for Callimaco, there is no common or national good that could justify his treatment of Uriah and Bathsheba. Nathan faults the biblical David, not for impurity, but for injustice, and the king admits his lack of pity. But Machiavelli ignores the personal and political troubles which the biblical narrative seems to connect with this incident. Perhaps Machiavelli's edited account of David means to suggest that the very greatest princes might ignore Aristotle's and his own warning about women.

Leaving Machiavelli's views of chastity, as seen through his version of the Lucretia story, we turn to a famous Christian commentary on the incident. In *The City of God*, Saint Augustine, upholding the value of chastity, exonerates Lucretia from any blame for having been overcome by Tarquin. Like the authors of the many medieval examples based on her story, Augustine asserts that a woman's most precious possession is her sexual purity. He recognizes that Lucretia was chaste in intention and was violated against her will. But he does fault her for her characteristic pagan attachment to worldly honor. Christian women, similarly violated, would suffer patiently and would neither postpone nor pursue death to preserve their reputations: "They have the glory of chastity within them, the testimony of their conscience. They have this in the sight of God, and they ask for nothing more."[28]

Machiavelli's Lucrezia begins as a Christian version of Livy's idealized Roman matron. She abandons the chastity of her namesake, but shares her pagan concern for honor. She lives to enjoy continued sexual infidelities with an untroubled conscience, but is careful to preserve her reputation, that is, the *appearance* of honor, as well. While both imitating and revising the Roman example, Machiavelli thoroughly rejects the Christian view.

Paul and Augustine preach the moral virtue of chastity because powerful sexual attractions, and even marriage, distract the Christian's attention from his primary concern with God and the eternal afterlife. If, to avoid worse distractions, one must marry, the marriage must be chaste. In a theology whose central notion is love, deviation and failure are aptly described as fornication and adultery. The great Christian poets whom Machiavelli's contemporaries revered depict love for a woman as an image of the divine love to which man's soul aspires. Dante's Beatrice is unattainable except in the life hereafter, and even there she is a temporary stop on the way to a love that no longer desires. This Christian view, reinforced with Renaissance Platonism, emerges as the ideal courtly love in *The Book of the Courtier*. The formulation is given after strict injunctions to faithfulness of wives to husbands, no matter how badly matched two partners are, [29] and after rejections of deceit in courtship:[30]

> Therefore let us direct all the thoughts and powers of our souls to this most holy light, that shows us the path leading to heaven; and, following after it and divesting ourselves of those passions wherewith we were clothed when we fell, by the ladder that bears the image of sensual beauty at its lowest rung, let us ascend to the lofty mansion where heavenly, lovely, and true beauty dwells, which lies hidden in the inmost secret recesses of God, so that profane eyes cannot behold it. Here we shall find a most happy end to our desires, true rest from our labors, the sure remedy for our miseries, most wholesome medicine for our illnesses, safest refuge from the dark storms of life's tempestuous sea.[31]

Machiavelli's remedy is a direct attack on the views that come together in *The Courtier*. Boldly, he introduces Callimaco as an outstanding example of "courtesy" (*gentilezza*). But the object of Callimaco's love is only a beautiful and virtuous woman. There is no indication that she represents anything more than that; he never speaks of her as the embodiment of a perfect ideal. Concentrating on "the things of the world" (*D.*, Intro. letter), Machiavelli abandons the quest for the City of God to speak about cities of men as they are, not as they ought to be. He follows Boccaccio's example in another new genre, and exalts the natural and present pleasures of sex.[32] He recognizes that most men must abide by sexual regulations as he means to avoid the related evils of striving and strife. Thus, the Romans were wise to forbid mere mortals to indulge in the philandering of Jupiter, and Moses's Decalogue prudently included a prohibition against adultery. But Machiavelli's play shows that, if one can indulge one's sexual desires secretly and with impunity, and even satisfy the desires of others in doing so, there is nothing inherently wrong with lust: purity is not a prime value for men or women. Part 2 of this chapter will continue to explore the relationship between Machiavelli's rejection of Christianity and his teachings about politics and sex.

Part Two:
A Preacher for Florence

One of the most interesting members of the conspiracy to invade and conquer Messer Nicia's domain is Frate Timoteo, who makes possible Callimaco's first evening with Lucrezia. Since Machiavelli's discussions of ancient Rome often include or imply radical critiques of modern Rome, of the principles and effects of Christianity, it is important to understand how his invention of this completely new character, a modern Christian priest, figures in this new version of the ancient story of Lucretia.

On May 17, 1521, when he was ambassador to the Friars Minor in Capri, Machiavelli wrote to Guicciardini how, while sitting on a privy, he had contemplated the preacher he would like for Florence. Just as he has never lacked a republic, at least in thought, so he can now imagine a preacher. But, as in his other opinions, he will be "obstinate," and his view will differ from that of the other citizens:

> They would like a preacher who would show them the road to Paradise, and I should like to find one who would teach them the way to go to the house of the Devil; they would like, besides, that he should be a man prudent, blameless and true; and I should like to find one crazier than Ponzo, more crafty than Fra Girolamo, more of a hypocrite than Frate Alberto . . . because I believe the true way of going to Paradise would be to learn the road to Hell in order to avoid it.[33]

The *stage* friar Machiavelli creates for Florence is indeed crafty and hypocritical. Under the guise of Christian piety, he teaches the road to hell. But in Machiavelli's play, neither the Frate's flock nor the Florentine audience to whom this road is shown is counseled to avoid it.[34] In fact, like many of Machiavelli's other works, the play does not seriously dwell on the existence of hell—or of sin, conscience, or immortal souls. Timoteo's traditional Christian authority is depicted as serving private and profane aims contrary to traditional Christian beliefs. He is described initially as an "ill-living friar" (*frate mal vissuto*); an audience would expect him to resemble the hypocritical friars so often condemned in Renaissance literature. But as the play progresses, the ends of his participation in the conspiracy are repeatedly referred to as "*beni.*" The good is now synonymous with the advantageous. By redefining "the good," Machiavelli's play rejects the Christian notion that "an evil man out of his evil treasure" will always bring forth evil.[35] A closer look at his Christians will show why.

Frate Timoteo's greatest influence seems to be with women. We first see him in a crowd of women speaking with one widow (III.3). As we soon realize, this widow's religious belief is really belief in the priest's authority, or belief in his beliefs. Thus, she asks in the same tone whether the priest believes (*credete voi?*) her husband is in purgatory and, shortly after, whether he believes (*credete voi?*) the Turks will pass through Italy this year. The latter question, which also reveals her frightened belief in rumors about Turkish torture, is one that amused Machiavelli when the womanish Friars Minor discussed it with him.[36]

But Frate Timoteo is no ordinary weak friar. Believing that "all women have few brains" (Ill.9), he manipulates Sostrata, who believes everything he says, and finally even Lucrezia, who doubts him. The only *man* who trusts Timoteo is Messer Nicia. Although he, too, thinks women are stupid, he is soft and credulous like them. As he gains "faith" in the false doctor Callimaco, Nicia says he trusts him as much as his confessor (II.6). Although Nicia is not a devout practicing Christian, he has been brought up in the Church and maintains an attachment to it. Machiavelli seems to suggest that Italian Christianity, along with Nicia's indolent bourgeois life, has made him impotent in more than one way and, therefore, subject to the deceits of more vigorous men.

Here, as elsewhere, Machiavelli indicates that the virtues, as taught by Christianity, appeal to and cultivate the feminine in human nature.[37] To Machiavelli, those like the friars, who might be said to have "made themselves eunuchs for the sake of the kingdom of heaven,"[38] are no different from women. Christian virtue thrives on peace and indoor activities, and teaches brotherhood and submissive obedience to authority. The strife that arises in modern times, like that mentioned in the play between Christians and Turks, or between Florence and France over papal alliances, is between conflicting religious parties. It may be especially fierce and bloody, but it is carried out in the name at least of future peace and love. Machiavelli sees these aims as unattainable and regards attempts to achieve them as likely to produce even worse disorders than the pre-Christian world endured. In place of this effeminate, even impotent, humane notion of human virtue and the evils it gives rise to, Machiavelli would substitute the vigorous *antica virtù* that he admires in the Romans. He would like to see this *virtù*—with all the implications of virility in its Latin root—born anew in his city.[39] This renaissance would be accompanied by an ardent love of liberty and independence, and by the ability to defend oneself and one's domain. In this renewal, the virtues taught by religion and treasured by the common people, especially women, would or would not be employed by strong men, according to their aims and circumstances.

Timoteo's first association with the conspirators is the abortion ruse. After this first test, he virtually contracts himself to cooperate with Callimaco and Ligurio. It is soon clear that Timoteo uses popular religious beliefs and fears to further his own ends. He pretends to the women that he learns how to act by studying books, but unlike Nicia and ordinary friars, he is familiar with the "things of the world." This is underlined by his allusions to time, which are surprisingly frequent for a man whose traditional focus might be expected to be on eternity.[40] Like Savonarola, Timoteo is crafty. Although he ceaselessly inveighed against the worldly-wise, the great Florentine preacher may, according to Machiavelli, have availed himself of their methods. Unlike the Roman augurs, Savonarola was a Christian and preached in an enlightened city. But like them, he gained the confidence of the people through references to supernatural powers. Numa claims he spoke with a nymph, whereas "The people of Florence . . . were persuaded by Frate Girolamo Savonarola that he spoke with God" (*D.*, I.11). Machiavelli does not comment further on the *truth* of the belief Savonarola inspired.

Timoteo, too, combines worldly *virtù* with Christianity. We *know* that his miracles are man-made. Like *mandragola*, they are contrived by astute men to manipulate beliefs and, thus, events, as they desire. Just as Callimaco's "remedy" works only because Nicia has faith in him, the Frate's miracles work because of his ability to inspire belief, faith, and trust. The connection between the success of "miracles" and the ability of the people involved is nicely presented in *Clizia*. At one point, Sofronia's credulous husband refers to the characters of *Mandragola* and to Timoteo's success when he prayed that Lucrezia might have a child. Sofronia, who prays for a miracle on her own behalf and then manipulates her husband's beliefs to insure that it occurs, knows how the Frate works miracles. Like other prudent and competent people in Machiavelli's works, he relies only on himself.[41] Like the Romans, Timoteo knows the value of religion that is "used well" (*D.*, I. 13, 14, 15). Thus, he recognizes that the reputation of a miracle-working Madonna depends on the friars, and that they have been lax. Repeating the words he uses about women, he remarks that his friars have "few brains" (V.1). For Machiavelli, the only miracle in Mandragola might be one like that referred to in his chapter on conspiracies in the *Discourses:* "When one [a conspiracy] has been kept secret among many men for a long time it is held to be a miraculous thing" (*D.*, III.6).

The debunking of miracles is accompanied by the parody or distorted use of religious language throughout the play. In the hymnlike

song to trickery, *inganno* is not only the "remedy high and rare,"
which Nicia supposes is *Mandragola;* it is also the means of true sal-
vation:

> you show the straight path to wandering souls; you with your great valor,
> in making someone blessed you make Love rich. You conquer, with your
> holy counsels alone, stones, venoms, and enchantments.

Similarly, the song after Act Four asserts that "holy" Night is the only
cause that makes souls blessed. The only *passione* in the play is the
one that makes Lucrezia sweat (III.11), and the adulterous "mystery"
is watched over by Saint Cuckoo and the Angel Raphael. Perhaps
Machiavelli is playing upon the angel's name, which means "*God
has healed*" (emphasis added).[42] The match between Lucrezia and
Callimaco, which is arranged by the marriage broker Ligurio, is
solemnized in church by Frate Timoteo. This solemn blessing and
Callimaco's consent to be the baby's godfather are further blasphemies
Machiavelli suggests in connection with his new preacher.

Timoteo must accomplish several seductions of his own to earn the
alms he desires. Like Machiavelli's men of *virtù,* he makes no attempt
to raise his parishioners to unattainable standards. He never exhorts
them to "be perfect, as your heavenly Father is perfect."[43] Rather he
descends to the level of Sostrata ("substratum") and uses her to attain
his purpose. Lucrezia's mother speaks often of her "conscience,"
which is eased as soon as the priest assures her that the proposed act
is not sinful. Like Callimaco and the "good companions" (*buon
compagni*) of the Prologue, she is a *buona compagna* (I.1) at heart.
She herself expresses the principle of choosing "the best among bad
courses" (*de cattivi partiti il migliore,* III.1), and advises her daughter
to relax and enjoy her evening. Lucrezia, however, whose nature is
alien to love (*le cose d'amore*) and amusements, requires a discussion
about sin and conscience. Timoteo's arguments are based on the
Machiavellian premise of no absolute good or evil, or as the Frate
says, "It is the truth that there is no honey without flies" (III.4).[44]
Early in the play he accepts Ligurio's argument for abortion because
the "good [*bene*] is what does good for the most people" (III.4).
Ligurio begins "I believe" and articulates a utilitarian definition of
good that replaces the moral virtues traditionally taught by religion.
This new credo is blessed by Timoteo and developed in subsequent
discussions with Lucrezia.

The Frate's rhetoric is calculated to lead her "to my wishes" (III.9).

He begins with the argument that strange and fearful things seem normal and acceptable when we are used to them (III.11). "As to the conscience," he generalizes that a "certain good [*bene*] is always preferable to an uncertain evil" (III.11). Despite his willingness to condone an abortion earlier, he now emphasizes the good deed of creating another soul for the Lord. Later, in private, he, too, seems uneasy about his actions, but again he rationalizes them by the "great good" (*bene*, IV.6) that will come from the evils of deceit, adultery, and his own desire for money.

With Lucrezia, however, he denies that the act is a sin. This belief, he declares, is a "fable" (*favola*). We might think here of the stories teaching that chastity is inviolable, like those in Livy, Ovid, or the medieval exemplary fables. At this point, Timoteo repeats some of the pleas of the original Lucretia's husband and friends, who beg her not to despair. Timoteo's argument that "the will is what sins, not the body" is almost a parody of the extended discussion of Lucretia's chastity in *The City of God:*

"A paradox! There were two persons involved and only one committed adultery." Finely and truly said. The speaker observed in the union of two bodies the disgusting lechery of the one, the chaste intention of the other, and he saw in that act not the conjunction of their bodies but the diversity of their minds. There were two persons involved, but only one committed adultery.[45]

The Frate advises the Christian Lucrezia that, since her will does not approve, she should willingly sleep with the stranger.

Timoteo does not differ from the other conspirators with respect to the conscience. Siro seems to have none; he'd enjoy seeing Nicia cuckolded as long as the dupers are not caught (II.4). Nicia never mentions his conscience. He regrets having to harm the young man, but is mainly concerned with discovery by the Eight, the Florentine criminal tribunal. Ligurio has no regrets before or after his trick. And Callimaco, though he briefly wonders whether he'll be punished in the hereafter, decides, like Castruccio Castracani, that there are many good people in hell (IV.1).[46] As in Machiavelli's more serious works, nothing need burden the conscience if one is not discovered in an immoral act. Only the imprudent have need of repentance.

Timoteo prefers another *favola* to demonstrate that "the end is to be regarded in all things" (III.1). This, of course, is a precept Machiavelli puts forth in *The Prince* while denying that there is any higher judgment for consciences to look to (*P.*, XV). The Frate's "end" is, as usual, quite different from the end to which Christians look. Timoteo cites the story of Lot's daughters in *Genesis* and argues that they were not disobedient to God and should not be blamed. Rather, they acted prudently, sacrificing their personal virtue for another end: the good, or the advantage, of the greatest number. Lucrezia has already told her mother that nothing could justify the adultery to her, even if she were responsible for the continuation of the whole human race (III.10). Her confessor assures her that, "because their [Lot's daughters'] intention was good, they did not sin" (III.11). He glibly approves of an act that biblical commentaries hesitate even to discuss. The narrator of the account in *Genesis* tells us that these incestuous unions between a drunken father and his calculating daughters produced the infamous Moabites and Ammonites.

In his depiction of Timoteo, Machiavelli takes liberties with the Christian Bible as well as with the Hebrew. His new preacher is not like the members of "new orders" such as the Franciscans and Dominicans (*D.*, III.1) who try to return to the original principles of their religion. Nor are his ends those of Savonarola who attempted, but failed, to restore Christian faith through "new modes and orders" (*P.*, VI). On the contrary, Machiavelli's new preacher seems to reject what his own religion stood for in its beginnings. This may be indicated in his name, which appears to be more than an ironic joke about his failure to "honor God." In the New Testament, Timothy is the recipient of two letters from Saint Paul, who describes him elsewhere: "I have no one like him who will be genuinely anxious for your welfare. They all look after their own interests, not those of Jesus Christ. But Timothy's worth you know, how as a son with a father he has served me in the Gospel."[47] Paul recognizes in Timothy a young man who will take up the Apostle's mission now that Paul is approaching his own end. What does Paul expect from the Timothys who will follow him? Most of the first epistle is devoted to the problems of church administration and the behavior of clerics. It also speaks at length of the modesty of women, especially of widows like the one Timoteo counsels in his first appearance. Although woman transgressed, she "will be saved through bearing children if she continues in faith and love and holiness, with modesty."[48] Finally, the letter contains the famous warning that "love of money is the root of all evils."[49] Machiavelli is well aware of the evils that originate in avarice, but his depiction of Timoteo and his discussions in the political writings make clear the differences between his attitudes and Paul's.

From his first appearance, to the last scene of the play, Timoteo is depicted in the act of receiving money. The Frate's desire for private wealth is not emphasized, for reasons discussed below, but the likely abuse of the responsibility to collect money for others is evident to Machiavelli, who repeatedly refers to the prominent place of greed in human nature. He is deeply critical of teachings and institutions that do little to mitigate the evils of human nature while ineffectively exhorting men to purify themselves in anticipation of an afterlife. The Frate's position shows what Machiavelli sees as a tension between prescriptions of otherworldliness and poverty on the one hand, and the injunction to minister to one's flock on the other. He also thinks that love of money need not be the root of all evils. The Frate's aim is clearly money, but in this play its use is not specified. Timoteo's continuing personal good depends on the good of his parishioners, and so he aims at a Machiavellian arrangement of mutual self-interest: some of the money *will* be used to maintain belief by acts of charity. Thus, Machiavelli suggests that Timoteo's love of money may result in some goods—though not in Paul's sense—as well as evils. The same would be even more true of unfettered political leaders in uncorrupt states. While avoiding the amassing of private fortunes and the concomitant growth of faction, luxury, and indolence, a prudent leader *can* guide his state to glory and power by the judicious management of money and men's love for it.

Mandragola should also be read in conjunction with Paul's second epistle to Timothy:

> But understand this, that in the last days there will come times of stress. For men will be lovers of self, lovers of money, proud, arrogant, abusive to their parents, ungrateful, unholy, inhuman, implacable, slanderers, haters of good, treacherous, reckless, swollen with conceit, lovers of pleasure rather than lovers of God, holding the form of religion but denying the power of it. Avoid such people. For among them are those who make their way into households and capture weak women, burdened with sins and swayed by various impulses, who will listen to anybody and can never arrive at a knowledge of the truth.[50]

Machiavelli's Timothy is an instrument and ally of "such people" and he knowingly ignores the epistle's advice to the soldiers of God "not to get entangled in civilian pursuits."[51]

Machiavelli gives us revised versions of characters from old books. Perhaps his boldest innovation is his presentation of an unholy family in the act of conception. Instead of a divine lover who "took our infirmities, bore our diseases" by fathering a baby,[52] we see a cunning "doctor" visit a chaste wife's bed at night under cover of the grotesque *mandragola* story, leaving the participants feeling "reborn" the next morning. In Machiavelli's renaissance and renewal, men who know this world rely on themselves alone, not on hopes of being saved.[53]

Those who believe that Machiavelli was a believing Christian will question the identification of Timoteo with his creator. Such readers might protest that the distortions of religion by a stage character are not Machiavelli's and that the author is attacking only institutional corruption and not the principles of the religion itself. They might remind us that thoughtful readers of dramatic dialogue always assume that no character is speaking for the author; relaxing this assumption would be like attributing to Molière the casuistic blasphemies of Tartuffe, something Molière goes to great lengths to deny in his defensive and moralistic preface to that play. But, as we have seen, Machiavelli is curiously unassertive about the conventional moral lessons to be drawn from this play. He does not claim—because he cannot—as Molière does, that he has removed all that might confuse good with evil.[54]

Like Ligurio, Timoteo is introduced as a familiar stock character. But just as the conventional parasite metamorphoses into a version of Machiavelli's *capitano*, Timoteo turns out to be like Machiavelli's projected preacher for Florence. The *frate mal vissuto* of the Prologue is *not* presented as an evil and disgusting example to alienate the audience. Compared to his brother friars in the works of Machiavelli's contemporaries, Timoteo is remarkably reserved. For example, there is no indication that the Frate enjoys luxurious food and clothing or women, and he is scrupulous about performing his formal duties. Productions that present him as a repulsive sensualist who paws Lucrezia, misunderstand Machiavelli's intent. He is not like Boccaccio's Frate Alberto; nor is he an Italian model for Tartuffe. George Meredith thought that "The Frate Timoteo of this piece is only a very oily Friar compliantly assisting an intrigue with ecclesiastical sophisms (to use the mildest word) for payment."[55] But, as we have seen, he is shrewder and more self-controlled than the usual Tartuffes, and, as a result, he is a far greater threat to the religion he professes; for, like Ligurio, what he really wants is not bodily pleasure, but money and the satisfaction of manipulating his fellow beings.

Although Machiavelli is amused at his friar's hypocrisy, and recognizes that the Frate is used by better men, he does share the *credo* articulated by Ligurio and affirmed by the Frate. This is evident from the song about trickery which immediately follows Timoteo's long discussion with Lucrezia in Act Three. The song is Machiavelli's: it comes between the acts as a comment on the action. The remainder of this essay will be devoted to Machiavelli's role as a teacher of youth and to his use of *comedy* as a vehicle to instruct the audience in the ways of Timoteo and Ligurio.

Part Three:
Comedy, Morality, and the Young

Like the Platonic Socrates and like Saint Paul, Machiavelli is, in his political writings, self-conscious and explicit about his relationship to the young. His aim is to substitute his teachings of "new modes and orders" for the teachings of earlier writers. *The Prince* and the *Discourses* are written treatises. Although they differ in form, magnitude, and emphasis, they are alike in that they are books with public subjects which are addressed to readers who will study them privately. The busy young ruler to whom Machiavelli dedicates *The Prince* read this short terse handbook and learn the Machiavellian mode of acquiring and maintaining a state. The longer and more rambling *Discourses* are dedicated to two friends of the author, young gentlemen worthy to be princes, who will peruse the volumes at their leisure. Machiavelli's stated intention is to inspire these readers to carry his project to its "destined place" (*D.*, I. pref.). In the introduction to the second book, he hopes to excite the minds of the young who will outlive him:

> For it is the duty of a good man to teach others that good which, through the malignity of the times and of fortune, he has not been able to perform; so that, many capable ones hearing of it, some of them, more loved by heaven, might be able to perform it. (*D.*, II. intro.)

These political books are also, in a way, *about* the young, since youth and vigor, although they do not guarantee *virtù*, are likely to be accompanied by it. Machiavelli says that Fortune, which always figures in the outcome of events, is "the young man's friend" (*P.*, XXV), and he admires "those who had the honors of triumph when very young men" (*D.*, I.600).

Mandragola differs from the treatises in being a publicly presented work with a private subject. The hostile Prologue, as Guicciardini suggested, says more about the author than about his audience,[56] and cannot be considered a dedication. But the identity of this audience is of the utmost importance in understanding Machiavelli's intent. Insofar as *Mandragola* has the same aim as the political writings, it too is addressed to the young, to those who are not yet fully formed. Machiavelli's audience is composed of young gentlemen, like Buondelmonte and Rucellai of the *Discourses,* who frequented the social and cultural gatherings in the courts and great houses of Italian cities. In Urbino, they participated in soirées of the sort depicted in Castiglione's *Courtier;* in Florence, they gathered for discussions with Marsilio Ficino in the court of Lorenzo de' Medici, or, more recently, with Machiavelli himself in the Rucellai gardens. And they attended productions of Roman and contemporary plays. In extreme contrast to the Athenian theater, which was financed and supervised as a civic event for the whole city and its visitors, these court productions were financed and presided over by *private* patrons like the Duke of Ferrara for a small number of invited guests, often for a private celebration like the wedding of Lucrezia Borgia. They took place in "small, ornate, secluded halls, removed not only from external nature, but from the view, indeed even from the consciousness, of all but those selected few who were permitted to enter them."[57]

Mandragola is not intended directly to reach the public at large. But the particular coterie to whom the play is addressed is one whose attitudes and future actions will have the greatest effect on the wider community. For these elite young gentlemen are the future princes or, in the right circumstances, the future republican leaders, of Italy. The circumstances under which Machiavelli wrote make all his writings political events. What he says must always be considered in the context of what he *could* say. It is thus necessary to pay the utmost attention to the sources to whom he attributes his teachings, that is, to the dramatic characters in his political books. The genre of *Mandragola* makes it the most public of his attempts to teach the young.[58] It also permits Machiavelli to say everything, for in a drama, the author himself says nothing.

Machiavelli's concern with the young is especially evident in *The Art of War,* which should be considered with *Mandragola.* Like the play, it is a dialogue in which the author never speaks. These two dramatic works are vehicles for the same principles Machiavelli sets forth in the political books, but their forms make these teachings more palatable, and hence, more publishable. In the lightest and in the gravest pursuits, the core of Machiavelli's teachings about justice is commonly acknowledged: all's fair in love and war. In the political books, not published during the author's lifetime, we learn that the true prince is as self-serving as a lover and as ruthless as a military *capitano*.

The Art of War is a technical handbook; its comments on Christianity, justice, and leadership are absorbed as the reader pores over military stratagems. The dialogue is clearly concerned with the young. Old Fabrizio Colonna converses in the Rucellai gardens with elite young men who will learn from him to revive ancient military practices. Like Machiavelli, Fabrizio won't live to see the enterprise through. The youngest questioner wishes to see the imagined army in action. Fabrizio's exchanges with him seem to parody Socrates' discussions with other young men about an imagined city: Fabrizio's projections are realizable.

The Art of War, like *Mandragola*, makes clear that love is an activity inferior to war. Cosimo Rucellai wrote love poems until Fortune would lead him to "higher activities." The form of the dialogue seems to parallel that of Boccaccio's *Decameron:* in a ravaged and suffering Italy, worthy young people retire to a garden for conversation, taking turns at "absolute power." Machiavelli's version replaces the theme of love with that of war. There are no women in the Rucellai gardens, and the consolations of love are replaced by the remedy of military *virtù*.

Philosophers, poets, and political theorists have remarked that poetry is more suited to teach morality than is history. This is implied in Aristotle's statement that poetry is more philosophic than history; in poetry human events occur not by chance, but as they would in a moral and rationally ordered universe. In *The Advancement of Learning,* Francis Bacon elaborates on this view: "because true history propoundeth the success and issues of action not so agreeable to the merits of virtue and vice, therefore poesy feigns them more just in retribution, and more according to revealed Providence."[59] In the terms of his famous formula about Machiavelli, poetry depicts, "not what men do, but what they ought to do."[60] For Bacon, "poesy" is useful only as an expression of human customs, passions, and yearnings. He thus advises reading *history* as a practical guide for human action: "it is not good to stay too long in the theater."[61] Perhaps he might consider Machiavelli's theater an exception. For *Mandragola* is effective precisely because it depicts poetically—and universally—the material Bacon assigns to history: the world as it is, not as it should be according to philosophers, poets, and preachers. Thus, we are shown what traditional morality would probably view as a deplorable but "true-to-life" situation, clever men enjoying the fruits of their immoral actions. But Bacon's formulae, both about history and about Machiavelli, are misleading. The greatest histories *are* "poetic"; they do order events so as to draw universal, philosophic conclusions about them. This is true of Machiavelli's histories, or commentaries upon history. Furthermore, like these "poetic" histories, Machiavelli's "historical" poetry does not really abandon the attempt to set standards for human behavior. Rather, it substitutes new standards for the "merits of virtue and vice." Thus, we must explain further the poetic vehicle Machiavelli uses to make his "historical" views of human action the accepted ones.

It has been said that there is no place for tragedy in the works of Machiavelli.[62] His views of human *virtù* and Fortune preclude a world where pity, fear, and the recognition of divine justice constitute the proper human attitude. But Machiavelli is at home in the comic realm, both within his political writings and his avowedly comic works—dramatic, narrative, and poetic. One effective way to undermine the sacred doctrines of older teachings is to refuse to recognize their seriousness. As Leo Strauss says, "If it is true that every complete society necessarily recognizes something about which it is absolutely forbidden to laugh, we may say that the determination to transgress that prohibition *sanza alcuno rispetto,* is of the essence of Machiavelli's intention."[63] But Machiavelli's "comic" *view* does not fully explain the way in which the genre of *Mandragola* is so well suited to his project. We must now return to the question of how Machiavelli uses *comedy* to teach the young as they watch *un giovane* seduce *una giovane*[64] from her older husband and from her old-fashioned morals.

Comedy and Morality

The greatest comedies in the Western tradition tend to conserve established "modes and orders." They may be critical of particulars—of timely fashions, government policies, the pretenses of the professions, the rigidity of age and authority—but they usually end by affirming the traditional teaching about virtues and vices that the older generation seeks to pass on to the young. Thus, in one type of intrigue plot the young lover and his supporters conspire to defeat or circumvent an opponent (often older) who would "usurp" the lover's place and interfere with his desires. New information, chance, the ability of the intriguers, and the stupidity of the opponents, accomplish what the audience recognizes as the appropriate and better arrangement: the enemies of youth are defeated, either reformed and reconciled, or punished and expelled. But youthful exuberance and passion must also accept limits, and so moral virtue is not really questioned. Individual elders may err, comically and with consequences, but the old *morality* emerges intact. A more satirical intrigue plot presents a conspiracy of clever rogues who prey on equally vicious or on foolish dupes. Here, too, the action may imply serious criticism of the established values and authorities, but, in the end, the play demonstrates the nonviability of deviations from the life of virtue.[65] In the plays of Aristophanes, Plautus, Terence, Shakespeare, Jonson, and Molière, these two intrigue plots—with modifications and variations—occur repeatedly.[66] In them, deviants may be loved and enjoyed, and even ambivalently admired, but eventually they are exposed and perhaps punished, and the rightful order is restored.

But this conservative effect is easily lost—through artistic shortcomings or by design. As a result, moral authorities have always been suspicious of the youthful intrigues of comic drama. Not necessarily, but not infrequently, comedy has been justly charged with subverting morality. The remainder of this essay will examine how changes in the traditional elements of intrigue plots enable Machiavelli to exploit some subversive *tendencies* of comedy in order to convey his truly subversive teachings. His intrigue plot is as different from those of conventional intrigue comedies as *The Prince* is from the conventional "mirror of princes" books whose form it resembles. Machiavelli's writings, both comic and serious, are still didactic, but what they teach is new.

As everyone knows, all good comedies end in marriage with the promise that the protagonists will live happily ever after. Happily usually means "in accordance with accepted morality," that is, virtuously. Machiavelli stands the comic convention on its head. His happy ending consists of the *subversion* of a marriage, of a successful adultery. "Who wouldn't be happy?" asks Sostrata at the end. Machiavelli's inversion of the convention of the comic theater goes hand-in-hand with his revision of the meaning of human happiness. Once again, virtue is replaced by *virtù*.

Comic Conspiracies

Readers of the *Discourses* know that Machiavelli thought carefully about what might now be called the "psychology" of conspiracies.

Readers of *Mandragola* have recognized, in the remarks of Callimaco, Ligurio, and Timoteo, key maxims of Machiavelli's teachings about conspiracy. The early acts of the play depict the formation of the conspiracy as new members are added. In comedy, Machiavelli employs an appropriate vehicle for his teachings because comedy often works by effecting a conspiracy outside the play, as well as within it. The physical seclusion and exclusion of uninvited outsiders from the Italian court theaters would heighten this sense of conspiracy. Bergson's suggestion that laughter functions as a "social gesture," assumes that members of an audience in a theater feel a common bond as they identify with some characters on stage and laugh at others: "laughter always implies a kind of secret freemasonry, or even complicity with other laughers."[67] The nature of the conspiracies that a playwright establishes (1) among the characters, (2) among the spectators, and (3) between the spectators and the characters on stage, is responsible for whether the play will have a conservative or subversive effect on the morality of those spectators.

The comic theater can be, as Bergson suggests, an institution that restricts immoral or unsocial deviations, as do the plots described above. On the other hand, comedy shares the power of all drama to make the audience identify with the characters imitated on stage, even if they would condemn them in real life. Thus, as Rousseau feared, stage imitations have a special ability to undermine morality:

> Let us dare say it without being roundabout. Which of us is sure enough of himself to bear the performance of such a comedy without halfway taking part in the deeds which are played in it? Who would not be a bit distressed if the thief were to be taken by surprise or fail in his attempt? Who does not himself become a thief for a minute in being concerned about him? For is being concerned about someone anything other than putting oneself in his place? A fine instruction for the youth, one in which grown men have difficulty protecting themselves from the seductions of vice! Is that to say that it is never permissible to show blamable actions in the theater? No; but in truth, to know how to put a rascal on the stage, a very good man must be the author.[68]

The tendency to be drawn into the play is especially strong in intrigue comedies because the spectator is so often invited to identify with a successful *group*, rather than with an outstanding but isolated and doomed individual, as in tragedy.

> Tragic actors expect to be applauded as well as comic ones, but nevertheless the word "plaudite" at the end of a Roman comedy, the invitation to

the audience to form part of the comic society, would seem rather out of place at the end of a tragedy.[69]

Comedy is capable of both greater social and moral "affirmation" (the spectator vicariously participates in the *group* reconciliation and celebration of accepted values), *and* greater "subversion" (the spectator identifies with a *group* that successfully celebrates its rejection of those values).

Returning now to the play itself, we can see that Machiavelli's views about human nature and politics are responsible for his revisions of the conventional conspiracy plot. These revisions are, in turn, responsible for differences in audience response, and, thus, for the Machiavellian subversion. This is evident in his depiction of the intriguers and their success, and his depiction of the duped—the objects of the intrigue—as well.

In his comic intriguers, Machiavelli makes attractive what would ordinarily be condemned as immoral. Callimaco is young, handsome, vigorous, and intelligent. Macaulay's objections to the comedies of Wycherly and Congreve is apt here, since the writers for the English Restoration stage sometimes used—or abused—some of the same comic elements as Machiavelli. Referring especially to their subversive attitudes toward "conjugal fidelity," Macaulay argues that "morality is deeply interested in this, that what is immoral shall not be presented to the imagination of the young and susceptible in constant connection with what is attractive."[70] Conservative comedies often present an attractive young hero who embraces immoral schemes to satisfy immoral desires. But, as I shall suggest below, in these comedies, our potential sympathy for such actions and passions gradually undergoes a metamorphosis. For example, either the hero's (and our sympathetic) initial fancy or lust is discredited by laughter or punishment, or it is controlled and transformed into a more spiritual and legally sanctioned love. Neither of these things happens in *Mandragola*.

Machiavelli's conspirators defy a distinction often made in comedies between "well- or ill-intentioned" rogues.[71] They most resemble the sympathetic schemers of a plot such as that of *Cassina/Clizia*. However, in *Mandragola*, the young dupers are not the rightful opponents of a would-be usurper, but, as I have suggested, the usurpers themselves. Thus, like Volpone and Mosca in Jonson's play, they are underminers of morality. The merging of the two intrigue plots described above and exemplified here by *Cassina* and *Volpone*, leads the audience to approve of Machiavelli's attractive conspirators. There is no conventional "poetic justice" in *Mandragola*. According to Machiavelli, justice is not a primary consideration, except insofar as it, too, might contribute to success. Machiavelli's rogues are eminently successful and thus are never exposed and punished. Their success, as I have suggested, depends on their benefiting others. Thus, although the conspirators are subverters of morality, they are not conventionally vicious, that is, ill-intentioned.[72] If comedy supports morality by making us angry at (or at least contemptuous of) the right things—by sharpening our sense of justice—Machiavelli's comedy deliberately undermines morality. We experience nothing like our desire to see the tripping up of such archdeceivers as Molière's Tartuffe, Jonson's Volpone and Mosca, or even more sympathetic deviants like Malvolio or Falstaff. Nor do we feel our initial relish for the intrigue turn to contempt, as we do for Boccaccio's comic (though unstaged) Frate Alberto. The conspiracy succeeds completely and there is no suggestion, like those found repeatedly in Jonson's didactic comedies, that the partners will defeat themselves.

Some readers have thought that Machiavelli's plays exhibit the successful maneuverings of clever people in order to help those who witness them learn to protect themselves. The printer of the first edition of *The Prince* suggested something similar when he sought Church protection against those who "do not know that those who instruct in the use of herbs and medicine, also instruct in poisons, in order to know how to guard against them." This would seem to be the intent of traditional moral fables, such as Aesop's or La Fontaine's, which often present a simplified narrated version of tricks like these in the intrigue comedies. But the fables, like some comedies, run the risk of misteaching—precisely because the schemer is attractive and goes unpunished. In *Émile*, Rousseau discusses the didactic effect of these stories on the "very young." According to Rousseau, the problem with La Fontaine's engaging fables is that they have the effect, if not the intention, of encouraging the young to identify with the successful fox, ant, or lion. Furthermore, since fraud is more admirable than force, when a clever gnat defeats a lion, the child's sympathies will be with the gnat. This, I believe, is the *intended* effect of *Mandragola*, and it is well described by Rousseau: "You are teaching them how to make another drop his cheese, rather than how to keep their own."[73] Unlike Jonson, whose moral lesson requires the humiliation and punishment of Volpone, the Fox, Machiavelli openly advertises elsewhere (*P.*, XVIII) that he is teaching the "virtues" of the fox (and the lion). Machiavelli's fox is, of course, much more prudent than Jonson's.

The injunction to develop subhuman characteristics is accompanied by the celebration of Chiron the centaur, identified by Machiavelli as the teacher of Achilles (*P.*, XVIII), and, we might add, of Asclepius the physician. Machiavelli, who in the dedication to *The Prince*, presents *himself* as the teacher of princes, seems to identify his teachings with those of Chiron. The centaur makes no appearance in *Mandragola*, but he watches from the wings, directing the action from backstage. Whether or not Machiavelli was responsible for the frontispiece of the first edition of the play (1518), the picture it bears could not be more appropriate. A centaur stands before us. In addition to the conventional strung bow on his back, this centaur bears another bow with which he plays a violin. The second bow distinguishes him from the many centaurs of classical and neoclassical art, those imprudent half-beasts who rape women and fight wars over the stolen brides of others. He is Chiron, the pupil of Artemis and Apollo, who told Peleus a cunning way to win the elusive Thetis as his lawful wife, and who later became the tutor to the son of this union. Although the author of the play was known, this first title page does not bear his name. Instead, it bears what might be considered a personal emblem. The prudent use of arms is a central theme in Machiavelli's political writings. Here, however, the instruments of war are at rest, and the centaur concentrates on the instruments of love and of poetry, the violin (*lira da bracchio*) being a modern Italian improvement on the lyre of Apollo. As I have suggested above, princes can be taught remedies for the ills of their times through plays and poetry, as well as through political writings.[74]

Machiavelli's view of human nature is responsible for differences in our attitudes toward the conventionally *deceived* characters, as well as towards their deceivers. In most "conservative" comedies, the former are either virtuous and unjustly abused innocents, or vicious and justly abused rogues. In *Volpone*, the victims with whom we sympathize are superhuman personifications named Bonario and Celia. Similar characters often appear in plays whose authors emphasize their moral purpose. Even *The Country Wife* has its Alithea and Harcourt, hardly superhuman, but clearly exemplary by the end of the play. *Mandragola* strikingly lacks characters like these who, however pallid and weak they appear next to Jonson's and Wycherly's able rogues, invite allegiance because they stand for an uncorrupt morality.[75] *Mandragola*, as Robert Heilman remarks, "is sometimes called a satire, but it is hard to see it as such, for it includes no dramatic assertion of an alternative standard which would invite criticism of the mode of life depicted.''[76] Once again, the absence of such characters is not surprising in a play by a writer who rejects the traditional exhortations to imitate the superhuman as a standard for human beings. Machiavelli also omits—and in this he resembles Jonson—any characters who are virtuous but also intelligent and witty.[77] Once more, this suggests that intelligence means knowing how to be both moral and immoral, depending on the circumstances.

Let us now turn to the other victims of the standard intrigue plot, the rogues who are punished by superior rogues. Again, Machiavelli's view of human nature is responsible for changes in our attitudes. Though other examples would do, *Volpone* provides an especially revealing contrast. Jonson demeans the vicious duped, as well as the vicious dupers, by caricaturing them as subhuman beasts. Thus, the wicked Volpone and Mosca prey on characters named Corvino, Voltore, and Corbaccio. Again, it is not surprising that Machiavelli, the teacher of *virtù* rather than of moral virtue, never suggests that his characters are less than human, either in their moral or intellectual shortcomings. As far as I can tell, the word *bestia* (or its derivatives) occurs six times in the play: in reference to Callimaco's desperate plot (I.3), to women mismatched with inferior men (I.3), to Lucrezia's fanatic piety (II.6), to Sostrata who can be counted on to convince her daughter to cooperate (III.9), to widows without children (III.11), and to men without women (V.6). In the first and fourth cases, the "bestial" is embraced and put to use. In the third and last cases, the term refers derogatorily to human beings who refuse to "accommodate" themselves—another frequent phrase—in order to secure their comfort and convenience in this world. Machiavelli thus inverts the traditional sense of this term as he does others.

Messer Nicia and Jonson's Corvino both arrange for their wives' adultery and their own cuckolding. But the naturalistic characterization and almost affectionate tone of Machiavelli's play reveal a radical difference between the two comedies. Corvino is depicted as vicious and evil, while Nicia is shown to be simple and lax; Corvino is punished by the Scrutineo, while Messer Nicia not only escapes notice of the Eight, but is peculiarly rewarded. Machiavelli's neutral presentation of the anonymous Donna in Act Three, Scene One is another example of his refusal to condemn either forceful superior people or their weak inferiors as "immoral."[78] Human beings are neither all good nor all evil (*D.*, I.27). Lowering our moral expectations or standards makes us judge only in terms of *virtù*. In stage comedy, as in life, it is difficult to feel righteously hostile or vindictive toward people who lack ability. Justice does not require the punishment of stupidity and Machiavelli mutes Nicia's moral shortcomings. Thus, we only laugh at Nicia's simplicity. If ability and aptness to succeed are all that matter, we will support the conspiracy of the able.

Comic Misrule: Roman Comedy

One way in which many comedies depict the overthrow of the sanctioned rules of society without subverting these "modes and orders" by audience complicity in the overthrow is to indicate clearly the *temporary* character of the upset. The conventional "comedies of misrule" are related, however distantly, to the ancient Athenian Festival of Dionysus and to medieval Feasts of Fools and Saturnalian carnivals, whose function was to serve as an outlet and, ultimately, to *preserve* the order and hierarchy of everyday moral life.[79] This conservative function helps explain why they were sanctioned by Athenian and Roman officials and, later, though more uneasily, by the Church. The Roman comedies were included among the events in the official state holidays (*ludi*), festivals associated with the state religion, held in honor of the gods, supervised by officials, and presided over by magistrates. They were performed on temporary stages or platforms, which were erected on public ground before a temple in the Circus, or in a building used for public athletic events.[80] Like their Greek counterparts, performances took place in full daylight, and their audiences included a cross-section of the whole community. The stage sets typically represented a street with the exterior of one or more houses. The exterior wall of these sets was not penetrated; interior action was reported, as in the Greek plays, by messengers or other characters who emerged from within. Machiavelli retains this stage convention, but like others, in his hands, it tends to emphasize the differences between his play and his Roman models. For, as we have seen, by the end of *Mandragola*, reports from within have revealed the complete and permanent reversal of the views that Lucrezia—and probably the audience—had at the beginning. We are still looking at the same unviolated exterior wall, but our inside information has informed us that the *appearance* of morality—in private as well as in public affairs—may be only an appearance. As Machiavelli teaches elsewhere, the civic spectacle may be only a cover-up for what's behind the scenes.

Machiavelli seems to have given some thought to the political uses and consequences of carnival and its absence.[81] But his play differs greatly from Roman and Shakespearean comedies, which allowed nonparticipating spectators to experience vicariously the temporary release that the older festivals had provided. The nymphs and shepherds in the first song of *Mandragola* emphasize the permanence of their withdrawal from serious pursuits. As I have argued, the play that follows emphasizes a similar permanent "release" from the restrictions of ancient morality and the Church. A brief look at the Roman plays from which *Mandragola* is superficially descended will demonstrate what a distant grandchild Machiavelli's play really is.

In Plautus and Terence, there is much that is racy and vulgar, and the plays are populated with those engaged in irregular sexual pursuits. But the reader will find few plays that inherently undermine the strict Roman morality of the audience that watched it. Once again, chastity and grave Roman women serve as a gauge. Virgins do not appear on stage;[82] habitual sexual license is limited to courtesans and their pimps; rapes are committed but there are mitigating circumstances; maidens remain miraculously intact or are overcome only by force and are often married when their true identity is discovered. Young people who defy their elders—even when they are justified by the folly of these elders—are reconciled with them and recognize their authority. They often ask for pardon or forgiveness, thus admitting their misbehavior.[83] Young men grow out of their impulsive yielding to nature, and become responsible husbands, fathers, and senators. Slaves may trick their masters, but they don't demand their freedom; there are reminders that they may be punished after the plays end. The dramas are only brief releases from the stringent moral codes of Roman life, and rarely fail to affirm accepted notions of piety, filial duty, chaste conjugal love, and friendship. As Duckworth says, "the plots are basically moral; the good are rewarded and villainous or lustful characters (*leno, miles, senex amato*) are punished . . . all this is not very edifying, perhaps, but neither is it harmful to the morals of the spectators."[84]

Furthermore, the plays avoid the danger of corruption or more than a temporary desire for "misrule" in the spectators, by not presenting a too-naturalistic world with which these spectators might identify. They are set far from Rome in a place infamous for license. The characters are, for the most part, stock stage types rather than naturalistic individuals, and the language, too, is conventional and removed (music and verse). In contrast, as Carlo Goldoni recognized, the power of *Mandragola* lies in its naturalism. It was precisely this powerful naturalism in the service of dubious actions that made the admiring young Goldoni uncomfortable—even as he resisted his father's ire for reading such literature.[85] To those who would protest that the action Machiavelli's play presents is limited to the make-believe world of the stage, we might remember Macaulay's reply to Lamb's apology for the English Restoration playwrights: Machiavelli's setting is the audience's Florence, the people are recognizable, the language is natural, and "one hundred little touches make the fictitious world look like the actual world."[86]

Perhaps these generalizations about Roman comedy are more consistently applicable to Plautus, but they also describe most of Terence's plays as well. The one Latin comedy that most resembles *Mandragola* is Terence's *Eunuch*, in which a carefully plotted rape is described in all its ugliness and even rationalized before the situation is saved by the conventional marriage.[87] The play ends with an "adulterous" ménage-à-trois of a prostitute, her lover, and a braggart soldier who will unsuspectingly support them. Like *Mandragola*, the *Eunuch* seems to defy the conventional morality: it presents approvingly, situations that make us vaguely uncomfortable even as we comply with the request for applause at the end. Perhaps our discomfort is provoked by the inclusion of all the unpleasant details of the action. It is hard to know what Terence intended in the *Eunuch*; the play may be an interesting failure.[88] But Machiavelli's play *intends* to divide us from our conventional assumptions. To do this, it must avoid recognizing the unpleasant implications of its action. Its artistic—though not moral—superiority is indicated by our feeling *little* discomfort at the end. Interestingly, as Elder Olson points out, Terence's failure to remain within the comic limits are related to his "tendency to humanize the characters,"[89] that is, to naturalize.

Commedia Erudita

Many of the plays of Machiavelli's contemporaries adhered more closely than *Mandragola* does to the Roman plots discussed above. Others added to the more familiar settings and characters, new plots of cuckoldry and adultery, like those found in the popular novellas. From these plays, one sees clearly the way in which the comic *intreccio* (intrigue) plots arouse audience support for what would ordinarily be judged as base actions. One can also see how the same action is so much more vivid on stage than it is in the novella. This is not the place for a comparison of *The Decameron* and the plays derived from it, but one might begin by noting the effects of (1) the author's moral frame for the stories, (2) the individual narrator's comments, and (3) the difference between a privately read narrative account and a publicly viewed physical representation.

Although some of the *Commedia Erudita* plots have elements in common with *Mandragola*, there are important differences. As in the Roman plays, the success of *Commedia* intrigues is often due to chance. Although the plays are cheerfully lax about language[90] and approving of adultery, there are few articulate rationales for the behavior presented. They do not consistently exclude the moral point of view. Furthermore, the rambling structures and, for the most part, stereotyped characters, undercut the audience's identification. There is something artificial and mechanical, not to say boring, about many of these plays, and this keeps an audience at a distance. Because they are artistically inferior to *Mandragola*, they are less successful at undermining traditional values. Finally, like the Roman plays, they were performed on public platforms, in broad daylight, a light and visible entertainment for the whole community. Crude and heavy-handed, there is nothing undercover about them.

The Comic Project: Conclusion

There are still other ways in which Machiavelli encourages the acquiescence of the audience in his new case. In addition to amplifying our complicity in the plot and removing all suggestions that its values are temporary fictions, Machiavelli prepares us to accept his premises by offering more shocking notions in order to get us to accept less shocking ones. We, like Timoteo, are tested by the proposed abortion plan, which is then withdrawn. *Mandragola* is substituted for the abortion medicine and, like the Frate, we abandon abortion and accept adultery. However, one might wonder whether, once chastity, conjugal fidelity, honesty, and the other virtues that Machiavelli turns to matters of prudential judgment elsewhere, are reduced to mere "fables," one shouldn't accept the practical arguments Ligurio makes in favor of abortion as well. Given the principles of action and conscience articulated in the play, one also wonders whether any but a prudential argument would stand up against *really* killing a vagrant lute player if this would further the purpose of the conspirators. If the power of *mandragola* were not a fiction, and Callimaco and many others would benefit from one unfortunate sacrifice, Machiavelli's play might seem to sanction such a murder.

But *Mandragola* is effective precisely because the most unseemly consequences of the action are merely implicit. When Machiavelli makes his principles explicit in *The Prince*, readers are shocked and repelled. But comedy, by convention, is permitted to treat the most serious matters lightly. Comedy laughs at everything, and the audience laughs too. The same immoral teachings, now exhibited in the private realm, are less shocking. But as Machiavelli says in his "Discourse about Our Language," the concealed serious lessons of comedy are tasted only after the laughter in the theater has stopped. In *Mandragola*, these new lessons are underneath the ancient comic form and come into focus when viewed alongside the ancient historic subject. Machiavelli does well not to call attention, in this play, to the conventional didactic purpose of comedy, because what he has to teach is far from conventional; it is truly "a new case born in this city." In the Prologue, the alienated author says that he hopes "you will be tricked [ingannate]" as Lucrezia was. This seems to apply to the ladies in the audience. But by the end, the entire audience has been taken in. We have all looked; and because this is a *play*, we have looked *together* as part of the conspiracy. By taking us into the plot, the author insures that we have been taken in by his teachings. Our applause at the end in response to Timoteo's "farewell" is also a response to Sostrata's immediately preceding rhetorical question, "Who wouldn't be happy?" Happy to applaud the happy ending, we endorse as a community a new notion of happiness. Machiavelli, the undercover captain in a new campaign against the old teachings, is an articulate preacher of *verità effettuale*. As the most eloquent seducer in his comedy *Mandragola*, he administers a remedy for the illness of the present age. And the remedy is administered as pleasant entertainment in a small, private theater.

Notes

1. Niccolò Machiavelli, Letter to Guicciardini (October 16–20, 1525), *Lettere*, a cura di Franco Gaeta, (Milan, 1961), p. 438.

2. Machiavelli, Letter, p. 439.

3. Machiavelli, Letter, p. 439–40.

4. For introductory surveys of contemporary Italian comedy, see Marvin T. Herrick, *Italian Comedy in the Renaissance* (Urbana, Ill., 1960) and Douglas Radcliff-Ulmstead, *The Birth of Modern Comedy in Renaissance Italy* (Chicago, 1969).

5. *The Prince*, ded., XV, XXVI and *The Discourses*, ded., I.intro., II.intro., III.1, hereafter cited as *P.* and *D.*

6. *D.*, I.intro.refers to sculpture, law, medicine, and government. One wonders why he omits drama. Elsewhere one of his speakers says, "This land seems to be born to raise up dead things, as she has in poetry, painting and in sculpture." See "The Art of War," in Machiavelli, *The Chief Works and Others,* trans. Allan Gilbert (Durham, N. C. , 1965), II, 706. See also "History of Florence," *Chief Works,* III, 1233.

7. See also *P.,* VI. These and other passages suggest that Machiavelli considers himself a political founder of some sort.

8. "Clizia," Niccolò Machiavelli, *Opere Letterarie,* a Cura di Luigi Blasucci (Milano, 1964), p. 71.

9. See Martin Fleisher, "Trust and Deceit in Machiavelli's Comedies," *Journal of the History of Ideas* (July, 1966), p. 370.

10. "Discorso o Dialogo Intorno Alla Nostra Lingua," *Opere Letterarie,* p. 225.

11. The story of Lucretia is told also by Ovid in *The Fasti* for February 24, and by Boccaccio in his *De Claris Mulieribus,* with which Machiavelli might have been familiar. Variants of the incident are found in contemporary works like Boccaccio's *Decameron* (II, 9). English readers will know Shakespeare's version of Lucretia and will recognize it as the source of the subplot of *Cymbeline* which refers to it explicitly. But in Boccaccio's story and in Shakespeare's play, the woman is not actually taken. The name of Machiavelli's heroine points to Livy's Lucretia rather than Boccaccio's, despite similar elements.

12. Livy, trans. B. O. Foster (Cambridge, Mass., 1967), I, p. 199.

13. Livy, I, p. 201.

14. Leo Strauss suggests that Machiavelli named him after the Athenian general Nicias, whose Sicilian campaign failed, in part, because of this superstition. In discussing the general, Machiavelli does not explicitly mention this quality. See *Thoughts on Machiavelli* (Seattle, 1969), p. 284; Thucydides, *The Peloponnesian War,* VII, pp. 50 ff. and 86; and D., I. 53 and III.16.

15. The songs were composed for a production of the play at Faenza or Modena in 1526. Unlike some readers, I assume that Machiavelli considered them relevant to the play, despite their later composition.

16. Theodore Sumberg, "*La Mandragola:* An Interpretation," *The Journal of Politics* 23, (1961), p. 322. This article came to my attention after most of the present essay was written. Sumberg takes the play seriously and reads it in the context of Machiavelli's other works. However, by drawing too close analogies between the play and the political works, he fails to explain adequately the function of the drama for Machiavelli. Nevertheless, he touches on many key issues.

17. See, for example, Plautus's *Phormio.* In some of the Roman plays, the clever slave or parasite seems to personify Reason in the service of his master's passion.

18. See *Mandragola* (I.1; Song after the first act; IV.9) and *Clizia* (I.2).

19. The evil character of the plot is referred to only once by Ligurio: "As if God granted grace in evil things as well as good ones!" (II.2). By the end of the play, it would seem that "God's grace" is irrelevant.

20. See Strauss, p. 343 (notes) for a list of relevant passages without reference to the play.

21. *P.*, XIX and *D.*, III.,6.

22. Baldesar Castiglione, *The Book of the Courtier* (III.44), trans. Charles S. Singleton (Garden City, N.Y., 1959), p. 248.

23. Lest the reader be misled by the following discussion, the context should be noted. Machiavelli completes the sentence with a reference to an earlier chapter (III.6) in which he discusses, not the breaking up of concluded marriages like Nicia's, but the breaking off of planned ones. See also Aristotle, *Politics*, 1311a, 1314b.

24. Livy, II.,145.

25. Aristotle, *Nichomachean Ethics*, 1107a. See also the references to adultery in the discussion of justice in book 5.

26. Livy, I., 37–39.

. 27. *P.*, XIII and *D.*, I.19 and 26. David's adultery is one of the two principal examples in Machiavelli's "Exhortation to Penitence," *Chief Works*, I.173–74.

28. Augustine, *Concerning the City of God against the Pagans* (I.19), trans. Henry Bettenson (England, 1972), pp. 28–29. See also II.17, pp. 66–67, for Augustine's comments on the rape of the Sabines.

29. Castiglione (III.55), p. 261.

30. Castiglione (III.70), p. 275.

31. Castiglione (IV.69), p. 355.

32. As Erich Auerbach says, Boccaccio also exalts a new doctrine of "love and nature" over the medieval ethic of love as "the mother of all virtue and everything noble in man." But Boccaccio's rejection of the medieval view is inadequate because the new order he substitutes for it is incomplete. See "Frate Alberto," *Mimesis: The Representation of Reality in Western Literature*, trans. Willard Trask (Garden City, N.Y., 1953), pp. 177–203. Read by itself, *Mandragola* elaborates the Boccaccian view of love and nature, as opposed to the Christian courtly ethic. Read in conjunction with the political books, the play is part of a complete replacement, applicable to all realms of human experience.

33. *Lettere*, pp. 402–5.

34. See part 3 below.

35. Matthew 12:35.

36. Letter to Guicciardini (May 18, 1521), *Lettere*, p. 409.

37. See *P.*, VI and *D.*, II.2 and III.27.

38. Matthew 19:12.

39. See *D.*, I. intro. and II.2.

40. Charles S. Singleton, "Machiavelli and the Spirit of Comedy," *Modern Language Notes* (November, 1942), p. 585.

41. *Clizia* (II.3). In the extant version of *Mandragola*, the Frate does not pray for a miracle for Lucrezia, nor is there any suggestion of sexual misbehavior.

42. Raphael accompanies Tobias (in the Apocryphal book of Tobit) when he goes to claim Sarah as his wife. Raphael tells Tobias to burn the heart and liver of a fish to save himself from her demon lover Asmodeus, who has killed each of her seven other husbands on their wedding nights. This remedy drives away the demon and makes possible Tobias's marriage. In a prayer of thanksgiving, Tobias emphasizes his sincerity and denies any lustful desires. See Tobit 2–9.

43. Matthew 5:48.

44. See, in contrast, Nicia's instinctive rejection of "sugar and vinegar" in II.6.

45. *The City of God* (I.19), p. 29.

46. Machiavelli, "The Life of Castruccio Castracani of Lucca," *Chief Works*, II, p. 558.

47. Philippians 2:22.

48. 1 Timothy 2:15.

49. 1 Timothy 6:10.

50. 2 Timothy 3:1.

51. 2 Timothy 2:4.

52. Matthew 7:17; John 3:16.

53. See the language of the Exhortation, which ends *The Prince* (XXVI).

54. Preface to *Tartuffe:* "from one end to the other, he [Tartuffe] says not one word, performs not one action, which does not depict to the spectators the character of a wicked man and which does not bring out that of the true man of good whom I oppose to him." See note 73.

55. George Meredith, "An Essay on Comedy," *Comedy* (Garden City, N.Y., 1955), p. 244.

56. Letter to Guicciardini (December 26, 1525), *Lettere*, p. 447.

57. Marvin Carlson, *Places of Performance: The Semiotics of Theatre Production* (Ithaca, N.Y., 1989), p. 61. In chapter 2, *The Jewel in the Casket*, pp. 38–60, Carlson contrasts these secluded, private theater spaces with the large, free-standing, "monumental" public theatres that were part of the everyday visual experience of the ancient cities.

58. For a vivid depiction of the seductive effect of Machiavelli (and of those he seems to approve) on a promising and impressionable youth, see Maurice Samuel's engrossing novel, *Web of Lucifer* (New York, 1947). Somerset Maugham's *Then and Now* (New York, 1947) also conveys this quality. Maugham's novel makes *Machiavelli* the protagonist in a plot adapted from *Mandragola's*. On Machiavelli's intentions with respect to the young, see Leo Strauss's *Thoughts on Machiavelli*.

59. Francis Bacon, "The Advancement of Learning," *Selected Writings of Francis Bacon*, ed. Hugh G. Dick (New York, 1955), p. 244.

60. Bacon, p. 330.

61. Bacon, p. 247.

62. Strauss, p. 292.

63. Strauss, p. 40.

64. The Italian word order in the Prologue draws attention to the youth of the protagonists more than most English translations do.

65. See Northrop Frye, *Anatomy of Criticism: Four Essays* (New York, 1969), pp. 163–86, for a discussion of archetypal comic plots.

66. Shakespeare, although he wrote one Plautian comedy, departed from the Latin models and developed his own comic forms. In this essay, I have tried to use for comparisons examples from comedies of the Latin type—Plautus, Terence, and the *Commedia Erudita,* which Machiavelli knew, and, despite their ambiguities, plays of Jonson and Molière.

67. Henri Bergson, "Laughter," *Comedy* (Garden City, N.Y., 1956), p. 64.

68. Jean-Jacques Rousseau, *Politics and the Arts: Letter to M. D'Alembert,* trans. Allan Bloom (Ithaca, N.Y., 1968), p. 46.

69. Frye, p. 164.

70. Thomas Babington Macaulay, "Hunt's Comic Dramatists," *Critical and Historical Essays* (New York, 1923), pp. 414–15.

71. Elder Olson, *The Theory of Comedy* (Bloomington, Ind., 1968), p. 52.

72. There is a corresponding collapse of the traditional classification of rulers at the beginning of *The Prince.* Machiavelli does not distinguish regimes according to whether they exist for their own or for their subjects' benefit, but according to modes of acquisition.

73. Jean-Jacques Rousseau, *Émile,* trans. Barbara Foxley (New York, 1957), p. 79.

74. For a discussion of this frontispiece, and whether Machiavelli had authorized the first edition, see Roberto Ridolfi, *Studi Sulle Commedie del Machiavelli* (Pisa, 1968), pp. 25ff. Ridolfi speculates about the date and place of publication, the decorative border, and the title, but does not mention the picture.

75. Although this is not the place for such a discussion, one could argue that *Tartuffe* and *Volpone* are, in fact, deeply critical of Christian religion. But if Molière and Jonson have inherited even part of the Machiavellian view, they present it more warily. These plays may be critical of Christian values, but they are careful not to hold up for emulation the behavior that undermines those values.

76. Robert B. Heilman, *The Ghost on the Ramparts and Other Essays in the Humanities* (Athens, Ga., 1973), p. 160.

77. Shakespeare's comedies, which I take to be the greatest of the conservative comedies, abound in attractive, intelligent characters who are also moral. Such characters distinguish these masterpieces from the heavy-handed didacticism of eighteenth-century English sentimental comedy. *As You Like It* is the paradigm.

78. See the discussion of this Donna in Singleton, "Machiavelli and the Spirit of Comedy."

79. See C. L. Barber, *Shakespeare's Festive Comedy: A Study of Dramatic Form and Its Relation to Social Custom* (Cleveland, 1968) and Erich W. Segal, *Roman Laughter: The Comedy of Plautus* (Cambridge, Mass., 1968). See also Mikhail Bakhtin's *Rabelais and His World* (Cambridge, Mass., 1968) and my chapter 2 above. The "New Historicists," following Bakhtin, Foucault, Geertz, and others, have written much in recent years about "carnival" and its purposes in the Renaissance and Tudor periods. Their views aim to be subversive rather than conservative of conventional morality and establishment hierarchies.

80. Margarete Bieber, *The History of the Greek and Roman Theatre* (Princeton, N.J., 1961), p. 152.

81. On shows and carnivals see: Letter to Vettori, 15 January, 1513; and *History of Florence*, V.15, VI.1, VII.12 and 21, VIII.36. Also *History of Florence*, II.2, 17, 36, III.9.

82. Many of the early *Commedie Erudite* continued the Roman practice of not showing the virgin on stage. Machiavelli translated *Woman of Andros*, which had no *virgo*, and, in *Clizia*, calls attention to the fact that the audience won't see the contested girl. Appropriately, *Mandragola* boldly exhibits the girl, only to transform her original from chaste matron to adulterous wife—a category that does not exist in Roman drama, but which is standard fare in Boccaccio and some contemporary comedies.

83. Jonson's *Alchemist,* despite its controversial ending, pays lip service at least, to the need to pardon and forgive the wrongdoer. Whether the contrite admission of guilt is to be taken seriously is too long a question to discuss here.

84. George Duckworth, *The Nature of Roman Comedy* (Princeton, 1952), pp. 303–4.

85. See Carlo Goldoni, *Memoirs,* trans. John Black (Boston, 1877), pp. 71–72.

86. Macaulay, p. 414. Machiavelli's care to make this world familiar to his audience is often undone by translators who attempt to substitute contemporary equivalents to make it familiar to their own. Unless the whole play is rewritten, this practice would seem to obscure Machiavelli's intentions.

87. Augustine criticizes the play on the grounds that the young rapist justifies himself by citing the example of Jupiter. See *City of God* (II. 7), p. 55, and *Confessions* (I), trans. Edward B. Pusey (New York, 1949), pp. 19–20.

88. See Olson, pp. 82–85, for a discussion of this play.

89. Olson, p. 84. See also Goldoni on *Mandragola.*

90. *Mandragola* contains strikingly less obscenity, both in language and gesture, than most Roman or contemporary Italian plays. Bawdy language and overt sexuality are not the only indications of a corrupting influence.

4

Three Views of *Henry V*

Shakespeare, Olivier, and Branagh

Announcements that Kenneth Branagh was preparing a new film version of Shakespeare's *Henry V* invited speculation about what a production "for our times" might mean. Laurence Olivier had filmed the play in 1944. His widely acclaimed *Henry V* was indeed a play for *his* time: a full-length production of the source of the great patriotic speeches he'd been performing for British soldiers in camp entertainments earlier in the war. Olivier's film is a splendid, glittering presentation of England's seemingly miraculous conquest of France in 1415, and of the dashing young king who achieved this victory. Olivier carefully and intelligently edited Shakespeare's play, removing anything that raised questions about the motives for the invasion of France, about Henry's heroism, and about the unity of England as a nation. England was at war and fighting for her life; in 1944 and half a century later, Olivier's patriotic movie aims to make one applaud her earlier good fights.

What could Branagh offer English and American audiences after Korea, Vietnam, and the Falklands? What sense could an even more democratic and secular generation make of royalty and heraldry, clerical power and kingly ceremony? Would such an audience still warm to the great patriotic speeches after forty-five years of cold war? Would a pacifist, anti-war version even be possible? Or might Branagh intend to give us *Shakespeare's* play, restoring material cut by Olivier and, with it, all the darker questions Shakespeare raises about conquests, kings, and nations?

And how would the new version handle the shift from stage to screen? Branagh and Olivier before him have at their disposal cine-matic technology Shakespeare never dreamed of, and both directors call attention to their medium. The limitations of Shakespeare's the-ater—the "wooden O"—with its artificial stage props and costumes and a small cast of actors are spoken of explicitly in Shakespeare's Prologue/Chorus to *Henry V.* Readers might wonder why he mentions them in *this* play, but not in the other histories, both English and Roman, where the audience also must make imaginative leaps of time and place, and see whole armies in a small-scale stage battle. The answer lies in Shakespeare's interest in the theatricality of Henry's politics; *this* "prince to act" is an extraordinary *actor.* And, like Olivier and Branagh, Henry himself is also the self-conscious director, as well as the star actor, in his story. The two films interpret the star actor differently, and the difference has something to do with the ways in which their directors use that modern invention, the camera.

This chapter will explore these differences, comparing both film-Henry's to Shakespeare's original stage-Henry. The presentation of these three Henrys invites us to think about the presentation of political subjects in popular entertainment, and consequently about the politics of play-watching. The first three parts of the chapter discuss Henry's decision to lead his nation into war (Act One), the peculiar heterogeneous character of this nation (Acts Two–Four), and the unification of the English nation with France (Act Five). The fourth part returns to the question of the wooden O and the movies and asks how live theater productions and films—including videos that can be watched at home on television—differ from each other, both in their modes of presentation and in their political effects.

Prologue/Chorus

Olivier is more interesting than Branagh on the differences between the theater and film. He begins with a leisurely tour of Elizabethan London on a sunny afternoon. The camera actually moved over a model based on Visscher's famous picture. The aerial photography might have reminded English audiences in 1944 of their own newsreels of enemy cities pictured from above in this way, and perhaps also of what London might have looked like to enemy German planes.[1] The camera wanders over the Tower of London, river, bridge, streets, and Bear Garden, and then moves into the Globe Theater, where the flag is being raised to announce a performance: it is the first of May, 1600.

The audience streams in, exchanges greetings, and finds seats while the musicians tune up. Backstage, all is astir with actors preparing, prompter in waiting, and curtain ready to open. The Chorus is spoken by an actor in Elizabethan dress who enters to communal applause. The first few scenes film the play as it is performed in the theater. The formal, archaic language of these early scenes might be difficult for a twentieth-century audience to follow. The interplay between actors and audience and much of the crude comedy at the beginning of the film give them time to get used to Shakespeare's language before the main action begins.[2]

As the scene changes to Southampton at the beginning of Act Two, Olivier moves us out of the "cockpit" theater and into the real world. It is almost as if we've successfully done what the Prologue had requested, as if we have "pieced out" their "imperfections" with our "thoughts," and the result is the true-to-life filmed rendition of the rest of the action. The camera, unlike our "imaginary forces," really can show us hundreds of horses and men, and really can take us from the English court to "the vasty fields of France." The forties film studio can do Shakespeare better than the Globe could because the camera can better achieve the illusion of reality.

Branagh doesn't really compare the film and the theater. His Chorus, a film director in modern dress, enters the studio in the dark, holding a match. In contrast to Olivier's deliberate location of the theater in London, here there is no indication of where this indoor, darkened studio is located. Nor do we see the communal nature of the work done there. The director is a detached and solitary *artist* who has, apparently, finished his work, and there is no sign of an audience. While speaking the Prologue, he flicks a switch and floods the room with light, revealing the scattered props and scenery for *Henry V.* The lines about the wooden O and the limitations of staged plays are less striking here than in Olivier's film because Branagh thrusts us into the film from the very beginning. Aside from the brief remarks in the first Chorus, there is no occasion to compare the stage and film representations. The Chorus reappears to introduce the action at different times and different places in the course of Branagh's film. Many of the lines about the inadequacies of the theater are cut from the later speeches and some are heard only in voice-over. The Chorus is sometimes almost comical as he runs along breathlessly behind the soldiers, or peeks in at the main characters—always outside the action in his twentieth-century director's clothes. After the dramatic beginning, the Chorus is a minor element in Branagh's version. We shall return to the beginnings of the two films at the end of our discussion. But now, the play itself begins.

Part One:
England vs. France (Act One)

In *Henry V* we see the clergy before we see the king. Canterbury and Ely confer in one of those brief, private conversations that Shakespeare often uses before the first public court scenes in his plays. Their exchange reminds the audience that Henry's England very recently has been wracked by civil wars resulting from the deposing of Richard II by King Henry's father, Bolingbroke. In that "scambling and unquiet time," a bill was proposed to deprive the clergy "of all the temporal lands which men devout . . . have given to the church" (I.1.9–10). This bill has now been revived; if passed, it will deprive the Church of considerable wealth and power. The lands are valuable enough to support a whole new nobility, one which, Holinshed remarks, would be completely dependent on the king who creates it. This brief exchange is enough to remind us that Henry V's claim to his own nation is only a few years away from his father's usurpation. Canterbury and Ely calculate that, in exchange for their support for the French campaign, Henry will drop the proposed bill. Both Olivier and Branagh to an even greater extent, abridge the clerics' long discussion of the king's wild youth. In the play, they dwell on the "wonder" of Hal's seemingly miraculous reform, and on his "*reason* in divinity," "*debate* of commonwealth affairs," "*discourse* of war," and his "sweet and honeyed *sentences*" (I.1.43–50; emphases added). It's not just that serious, adult, political business has replaced the adolescent slumming of his youth. It's that his *speech* about such matters is noteworthy. This combination of carefully staged seeming "miracles" and extraordinary speaking abilities will characterize Henry throughout the play. Speech is the primary instrument of the king. In this he resembles stage actors. The cagey churchmen intend to manipulate the young king for their own purposes, but their first description of him indicates the ways in which he will rule them and the rest of his kingdom.[3]

Our first view of Henry/Olivier is of a rouged actor backstage in the Globe. He clears his throat, assumes his posture, and "becomes" Henry V, as he makes his entrance to the applause of his own court and the Globe's Elizabethan audience. The stage is brightly lit, Henry wears a red robe and a gold crown and enters confidently, in full motion. The camera remains distant enough to show him as a lively young star in the midst of an approving and sociable court. Although Olivier is an actor acting an actor who is acting the king, his Henry is such a good actor that he gives little indication that he is calculating every move for its effect. At the end of the scene, for example, note how casually he seems to toss his crown onto the post of his throne. Since we've seen the actor become Henry, we might suspect that Henry also may be playing a role. But once he gets going and we move out of the theater, he's a fairy-tale prince who holds our allegiance from beginning to end. We don't think much about calculated acting on his part. To us, as well as to his subjects, he appears a natural hero, comfortable and in full control of his court.

Henry/Olivier steps out of medieval manuscript illustrations or pictures of an Elizabethan court. His colors are red and blue, gold and silver; his materials are stone and shining armor. Henry/Branagh is different. He reminds us of Brueghel's browns, of a more northern world where mud and heavy cloth are the dominant stuff, where even the king is more down-to-earth. In contrast to Olivier's movie idol good looks, Branagh's somber, cruder appearance and slow entrance through the dark hall reveal, at every step, his calculating and careful self-consciousness. This Henry, too, must be an actor. He moves slowly through his nobles. The camera focuses on each one separately and each acknowledges him watchfully as he passes. Through most of this scene he sits still upon his throne, deliberately soliciting advice from the clerics. The camera focuses frequently on his own watchful, tense face, inviting us to wonder what he's thinking. But at this point, Branagh leaves us at the surface. Henry's new reign is in a delicate position, and it's not yet clear, to him or to anyone else, that the apparently reformed prince is up to the job. The camera increases our doubt by moving from individual to individual, rarely pulling back, as Olivier's does, to take in the whole court as a unified group. Shadows and dark places, as well as the broken space of the hall, suggest the separate interests at work. Repeatedly referring to God and to conscience, the king requests the clergy's opinion about the legality of the planned invasion of France.

The speech Shakespeare wrote for the archbishop of Canterbury explaining why Salique law does not forbid Henry's claim to France is long, windy, and difficult to follow. Before going to the movies, let us examine it carefully. Although it is offered and accepted as support for the English claim, this speech can't help but raise questions for the

attentive listener about the legitimacy of Henry's claim, and about the
meaning of the word "nation." To begin with, it's not clear whether
"Salique land" refers to France or to Germany, the latter being defined
by its geographical location between two rivers, and identified by the
name Meisen. What exactly does define a nation? Is it a natural entity,
determined by geography, birth, and ethnic ties? Or is it a conventional
and changeable artifact, the product of human action, will, and
speech? According to the Archbishop, Charles the Great, King Pepin,
and Hugh Capet all founded their titles on a "show of truth," but
really won the French throne by "subduing," "deposing," or "usurping." All appear to hold in "title of the female" as "do the kings of
France up to this day." Their "crooked titles" are all derived from
women; there is, therefore, no bar to Henry's claim to "inherit from
the female" (I.ii.33–95). The archbishop argues, in effect, that Henry's
claim is as legitimate as that of the French kings because it is based on
the same illegitimate principle. Furthermore, the invasion and conquest of France would secure Henry's claim by the same force the
French kings used. Of course, Canterbury does not say that Henry
would be subduing, deposing, or usurping, while depending on a
"show of truth." He cites one more authority, the Book of Numbers,
and ends with a rousing exhortation to Henry to "stand for his own,"
as his uncle Edward, the Black Prince, did in his campaigns. Here the
archbishop carefully relates Henry V to the legitimate English line. He
does not mention the legal successor to Edward, Richard II, who was
deposed from the throne by the usurping father of the present king. In
Henry V, there is no public mention of Richard, the divine-right king
who behaved as though God and the land itself would maintain him as
its sovereign, no matter what he did. Nor does Canterbury mention
Mortimer, the earl of March, who, by the archbishop's reasoning,
ought to have succeeded to the throne if Richard failed to produce a
male heir.

   Now let us look at the films. In Olivier's, the archbishop's speech is
given in full, but is accompanied by so much comic business between
actors, audience, and even Henry, that we hardly listen to what he is
saying, or we quickly dismiss it. The speech may sound confused, but
we don't suspect that it is deliberately devious. What could fusty old
arguments about international law add to the exuberant glitter and
energy of this handsome young king? Just as Bolingbroke's natural
ability to rule supplanted Richard's conventional claims to the throne,
his son's charm and confidence seem to justify his claim to France,
whether the archbishop sanctions it or not. The dauphin's insult

provides Henry with his first occasion for a rallying speech. This warm and rousing reply further unifies the court, which responds with enthusiasm.

Branagh's archbishop, in contrast to Olivier's confused and comic cleric, speaks slowly and clearly. Again, our attention is so riveted to the king that we don't really examine the speech. But the nobles laugh guardedly as Canterbury concludes that his argument is "as clear as is the summer sun" (I.ii.86). They know and we know that there is something wrong with his reasoning. Though Branagh's Henry is as somber and solitary as Olivier's is high-hearted and sociable, here, too, it is clear that his own nature matters more than legalistic arguments about his "right." Henry listens carefully, hears what he needs, and wills to take France. He has staged the proper consultation and now can turn to business. Branagh keeps the speech to the French ambassador tight and tense with the camera mostly on the king's face, not on the whole court. He speaks quietly, coldly, without changing his position, and deliberately shows his repressed rage. We may sympathize with the young king's position, but the terrifying delivery is not likely to inspire affection—in the court or in the film audience. At this point, we're mostly intrigued by who's using whom. The rest of Branagh's film will be devoted to making us care for this young man, despite the necessity that he be cold, tough, and even ruthless, at times.

Part Two:
Making a Nation (Acts Two–Four)

By the time Henry V becomes king, most of the repeated challenges to his father's rule have been squelched. These threats to the unity of England were from former enemies who opposed Bolingbroke's seizure of the crown and from former allies who aided him to it. Henry IV intended to reduce internal schism by directing the attention of the English to exploits abroad. Crusades—bloody wars in the name of God—would do double duty as penance for Richard's death and as a way of uniting factions at home. Domestic rebellions repeatedly interfere with Henry IV's crusade plans, but even on his deathbed in the "Jerusalem" room, he recommends the same strategy to Prince Hal, urging him to "busy giddy minds/ with foreign quarrels"(*2HIV*, IV.v.212–14). Neither film supplies any of this background, which would be familiar to Shakespeare's readers from the earlier plays.

Both films make it seem as though the French campaign is primarily an opportunity for the reformed prince to prove his ability to be king of England. The foreign policy calculated to strengthen a dubious claim even to his own throne is less evident. One especially feels the absence of the more political background in Branagh's film, since he so freely uses flashbacks to supply the more personal and psychological background of Hal's present situation.

In Act Two, Scene Two of Shakespeare's play, even before the English army embarks for France, the king reveals that there are Englishmen who would betray their king and country to the French. The foreign policy recommended by Henry IV is almost undercut before Hal ever attempts it. "Giddy minds" have betrayed the English war effort and gone over to the enemy for private gain. In 1944, perhaps at the urging of Churchill, Olivier completely cut this incident, to avoid any suggestion of a "fifth column" in England. Only the shipboard hymns and Henry's mercy toward the drunken man remain.

Branagh includes the entire Southampton scene, which he says Henry "stage-manages."[4] Characteristically, he emphasizes Hal's personal distress at his betrayal by a close comrade. After knocking him around, Branagh/Henry pins Scroop down on a table and, loverlike, expresses his outrage at the violation of a personal trust. The camera comes in very close to the two faces, Hal holding Scroop's head, excluding for the moment all the public witnesses of this private moment. The incident is important in considering how Branagh, later in the play, treats the king's dealings with his own former friends; at Southampton, Henry is the betrayed friend. He turns the public exposure of his private injury into a powerful occasion for reaffirming the unity and identity of England. Fighting "his natural human instinct,"[5] he orders the executions, claiming that God has brought the traitors to justice, and rerallies his "dear countrymen" to advance in his cause: "No King of England if not King of France" (II.ii.193). Here, as in the earlier council scene, Branagh keeps his camera close upon himself. And here again our attention is less focused on the countrymen he aims to unite, and more drawn to his private pain.

In Act Two, Scene Four, Exeter tells the French king that France's "borrowed glories" belong to Henry "by gift of Heaven/ by law of nature and of nations" (II.iv.79–80). The tone suggests that nations are made in heaven and that the two laws are coincident. But Canterbury's teachings about international law have already revealed a resemblance to the thinking of an earlier influence on King Henry V. In *Henry IV* ,

Part Two, when Falstaff decides to reacquaint himself with Justice Shallow, he muses:

> If the young dace be bait for the old pike
> I see no reason in the law of nature but
> I may snap at him. (*2HIV,* III.ii.341–2)

As we have already seen, Henry himself is willing to turn to "natural" compulsion if the "law of nations" is not complied with: "France being ours, we'll bend it to our awe/ or break it all to pieces" (I.ii.224). If the French won't yield to his supposedly legal title, he says that "bloody constraint" will follow and that "hungry war" will open its "vasty jaws" (II.iv.104-5). Nations, it would seem, are made—and unmade—not in heaven, but by men with the will and strength to make them. This is clear at Harfleur when Henry exhorts his troops to "disguise fair nature with hard-favored rage" (II.i.8). Holinshed calls attention to Henry's attempts to acquire France peacefully, to avoid the "effusion of Christian blood." He even mentions Henry's order forbidding the English to steal from churches, molest civilians, or plunder the villages in the vicinity of Harfleur. He frequently notes that Henry's harshest threats and deeds were necessary, or were exceptions to his usually gentle character. Shakespeare, in contrast, shows Henry's readiness to resort to brutal and ruthless force without indicating any reluctance or regret on Henry's part. In his ultimatum to Harfleur, the king is clearly speaking to his own men, as well as to the governor of the French city. He suggests and, in effect, *orders* the rape and pillage of the town if Harfleur doesn't yield. Olivier films the first speech about Harfleur, "Once more unto the breach," from above, using the camera to make the king look more like an underdog than a besieger.[6] Understandably, he completely cuts the terrible speech before the walls. Branagh restores it in full. He portrays Henry as willing, but *reluctant,* to use ruthless force against civilians. We should note here that Harfleur is conquered not by force, but by a forceful speech by the man who directs the action and plays the lead part. His Machiavellian ploy works, and the increasingly likable young king breathes a sigh of relief and sincerely orders his troops to show mercy. After the surrender, Branagh almost falls. Despite the terrifying Harfleur speech, his exhaustion,[7] like Olivier's high camera, makes him appear the sympathetic underdog. God appears to have taken the side of "Harry, England, and St. George."

What "England" means in the fifteenth century is still ambiguous, for England's ethnic identity has been problematic since the Norman conquest. The French refer to their English foes as "bastard Normans" (III.v.9). In addition, continual attempts by the English to conquer France raise questions about whether this other nation will remain other if England ever succeeds in making France her own. And will the English be recognizably English after the assimilation of France? The play presents them as recognizably distinct from the French, anachronistically ignoring the fact that fourteenth-century Englishmen looked and sounded much more French than Shakespeare and Olivier make them. Branagh, as we shall see, mutes the differences, not to be historically accurate, but to make both sides sympathetic. But Shakespeare draws our attention to differing language, dress, and holidays because he is interested in the question of national character. This question is complicated by another peculiarity of England as a nation.

Although she could be marked off geographically—as in John of Gaunt's famous speech in *Richard II*—England's natural (made in heaven?) island borders do not simply or permanently define her. The Channel, which Gaunt so memorably evokes as a physical and psychological divide or barrier, has repeatedly served as a highway for invaders, and Southampton, the scene of Henry's first internal betrayal, was often the port of entry. Olivier's audience would be especially sensitive to the island's modern accessibility in an age of air warfare, as Branagh's would be in the time of "Chunnel" construction.[8] England's peculiar ties to France and to Ireland are the causes of repeated wars. In addition, she has had to struggle with the repeated efforts of geographically connected parts of the island realm to separate themselves and to assert their national character and identity as autonomous nations.

In the history plays, England is continually flying off at the margins. Richard II loses his throne to Bolingbroke while attempting to suppress an Irish rebellion, and it is no accident that the Percys, whose realm is the northern margin of the kingdom, are the leaders of repeated rebellions. The Welsh leader, Owen Glendower, also at the edges, is marked by his stilted English and exotic claim of magical powers. He, too, is ready to support the rebellion of the lords who helped Henry IV to Richard's crown. It is questionable whether Glendower has much in common with his English comrades in rebellion, except for their common enemy. His daughter is separated from her husband Mortimer by an insuperable language barrier. This Mortimer, the earl of March, is another border man. He is supposed by the rebels to be

Richard's appointed heir to the crown. The earl of Cambridge, one of the Southampton traitors, was related to Mortimer. Glendower's fantastic claims about his supernatural powers are a continual source of irritation to the northern Hotspur, who looks less marginal whenever the Welshman is nearby. The first thing we hear about the Welsh in *Henry IV, Part One*, is of their barbarous treatment of prisoners of war (*1HIV*, I.i.43–46). Their status in the kingdom of a Christian king is questionable from the beginning.

The problematic identity of England as a unified nation if the rebels should succeed is most vividly portrayed in *Henry IV, Part One*, in the argument of Glendower, Mortimer, and Hotspur, who anticipate their victory over Henry IV by planning to split the country into three parts; Hotspur would even redo the natural landscape by rerouting a river to enlarge his realm (*1HIV*, III.i). Are these men fighting for a *nation?* At the end of the play, the English rebels have been subdued, but Glendower and Mortimer remain at large, active threats at the edge of the kingdom. Their ally, "the noble Scot, Lord Douglas," who is still part of an autonomous land, is set free by Prince Hal.

The *author* of *Henry V* is still very much interested in the question of England's peculiar heterogeneous identity as a nation. After obtaining the archbishop's sanction for his war on France, Shakespeare's Henry immediately raises the question of Scotland. Canterbury, as Holinshed reports, replies that the March earls will be a sufficient defense of England's northern border. But Henry persists:

> We do not mean the coursing snatchers only;
> But fear the main intendment of the Scot,
> Who hath been still a giddy neighbor to us. (I.ii.143-45)

Hal never got to consult his father about the Scots' giddiness, but whenever England turns to "foreign quarrels" and charges "once more into the breach," Scotland comes "pouring like the tide into the breach":

> For once the eagle [England] being in prey,
> To her unguarded nest the weasel [Scot]
> Comes sneaking, and so sucks her princely eggs. (I.ii.169–71)

Legally or morally, the "eagle" is indistinguishable from the "weasel," but its size allows it to attack openly. Under the guise of the "law of nations," each will grab what it can, following Falstaff's "law of nature" that big fish may eat little fish (*2HIV*, III.ii.340–42). Canterbury assures the king that those who remain in England will defend the home fires from outside attacks. Another solution that Shakespeare's late Elizabethan audience might have been thinking of would be to make what is "outside" inside; if Ireland and Wales can be English, why not contiguous Scotland as well? Ely thus argues:

> If you will France win,
> Then with Scotland first begin. (I.ii.168)

Assuring Henry that the entire kingdom will support him, the archbishop paints a pretty picture of "the rule of nature" and of an organic and thus naturally constituted "government," whose parts "work together in a full and natural close," like honeybees in a hive. By the time Canterbury gets to "many arrows coming to one mark" and many streams meeting "in one salt sea," the king has resolved to leave for France, and the Scottish weasel no longer seems a threat. But Shakespeare has raised the question, and it remains with us as we meet with the heterogeneous group of officers who follow Henry to France. Both Olivier and Branagh omit the Scottish question. The omissions are early indications of how both directors downplay the artificial character of the nation Henry is attempting to patch together. But Shakespeare makes it clear that Henry V's England cannot be the bounded isle and homogeneous paradise that the dying John of Gaunt conjured up in speech two generations before.

Act Three, Scene Two exhibits the four ethnic Englishmen for the first time. All speak English, but each speaks in a distinct regional—or stage regional—dialect. The peppery Welshman, Fluellen, is a legalistic soldier. He measures all military action by abstract rules about the "disciplines" of war, especially those of ancient Rome. He approves of the Scottish Captain Jamy, whom Shakespeare anachronistically includes among Henry's loyal officers. Fluellen says that Jamy can "maintain his argument as well as any military man in the world in the disciplines of the pristine wars of the Romans "(III.ii.82–84). But the Welshman has nothing but contempt for the Irish Macmorris, who wants action, not talk. Both Fluellen and Macmorris are sensitive about their origins. Their oaths—Fluellen swears "by Chesu" and Macmorris "by Crish"—presumably unite them on a higher level as Christians. But by the end of their quarrel, they are arguing about their worth as men. The last words of Macmorris, whom we do not see again, exclaim:

> I do not know you so good a man as myself;
> so Crish save me, I will cut off your head. (III.ii.134–35)

They cease going for each others' throats to join in their common cause as Englishmen. As Macmorris puts it, "There is throats to be cut" (III.ii.114). He means, of course, what Henry IV had suggested: foreign, French throats. After the victory at Agincourt, Fluellen reminds Henry V of the part the Welsh played in his "great uncle's" (he means his great-grandfather's) victory over the French at Crécy. Always the charming diplomat, the king agrees that he has always honored Welsh customs, and even embraces his own Welsh origins: "For I am Welsh, you know, good countryman" (IV.vii.108). In Olivier's film, this exchange is omitted. There is no indication of any tension in the English alliance. Owen Glendower is a danger of the past, and Fluellen's fuming about the "disciplines of war" are reduced to comic character quirks. In a charming scene at the beginning of Act Five, Pistol, who is English riffraff and has insulted Fluellen's Welsh origins and customs, is forced to eat a Welsh leek. The English officer, Gower, has the last word.

> You thought, because he could not speak English
> in the native garb, he could not therefore handle
> an English cudgel. You find it otherwise, and
> henceforth let a Welsh correction teach you a good
> English condition. (V.i.78–82)

Shakespeare's serious interest in the question of national unity as a political problem and in Henry's new attitudes to the law of nations is genially muted throughout Olivier's film. The scene with the four captains is "a comradely gathering of representatives of the four nations,"[9] an "interlude," an "episode removed in spirit and substance from the more serious main action." It is even filmed against a "painted backdrop."[10]

Olivier's genial treatment of the ethnic tension in Shakespeare's play was, of course, dictated by his own political aims: to contribute to the war effort by depicting a united England in an earlier time of stress. Part way through production he had to move his crew to Ireland so that filming would not be interrupted by military aircraft flying over

England. The Irish weather continued to pose problems, but in the completed film, it rains only once, with comic effect, on the Globe audience. Ireland was technically neutral during the war, though anti-English sentiment was responsible for some sympathy for Nazi Germany. You'd never know it from Olivier's movie. The film is dedicated to the "Commandos and Airborne Troops of Great Britain— the spirit of whose ancestors it has been humbly attempted to recapture." The last item of the credits reads: "Infantry and Cavalry by members of the Eirean Home Guard." Just as he eliminates the traitors at Southampton, so he softens ethnic hostilities and gives 1944 audiences a united front under a sunny sky. War-torn Britain could not have stood anything else.

Branagh, too, draws little serious attention to the ethnic diversity that Shakespeare included and Olivier muted. Branagh lived in Belfast until he was nine years old. In the *English* English he has cultivated since then, there is no trace of the thick brogue of his early years, though his strikingly Irish looks remain. Indeed, they are especially prominent in all those facial close-ups. But his film does not emphasize the question asked by the one Irishman in this English history play. Macmorris, goaded by the talkative Fluellen, asks with increasing irritation, in his stage Irish accent, "What ish my nation?" (III.ii.124). After the bloody confusion of battle, the "exhausted," boyish king breaks down, unable to prevent his tears,[11] and hugs Fluellen in relief that there is still any possibility of human fellowship in this world. There is no indication that King Henry may find it useful to assert his Welshness after this battle. The scene is heartwarming and moving, but, like Olivier's, it is less interesting than Shakespeare's on the political strategies of Henry V. In the end, once again, Branagh seems more interested in psychology than in politics, in friendship than in leadership.

We see this also in Branagh's depiction of the lower-class riffraff who cease their own brawling in Act One to follow King Henry as "three sworn brothers to France" (II.i.13). Pistol is the central figure among them. We also know the others from the earlier plays, as the companions of the king's younger, wilder days. Though they must be excluded from the king's personal affairs, they, too, are Englishmen and must be integrated into the nation Henry is forging. Branagh's flashbacks to the Boar's Head Tavern splice together lines from the two earlier plays. Some are shifted to different characters; all aim to heighten Hal's pain at having to sever these old ties. In one of the most beautiful and moving scenes in the film, Branagh depicts Falstaff's friends—Mistress Quickly as the centerpiece—as they remember the old knight and then part forever. By the end of the play, Bardolph has been executed, and Mistress Quickly and Falstaff's boy are dead. Pistol, who goes to France to "suck" (Shakespeare uses the word he used about the Scottish "weasel"), is left humiliated and alone. He exits, planning to "steal" back to England—where he plans to "steal" (V.i.90). Though Holinshed reports that Sir John Falstaff was made a lieutenant at Harfleur, Shakespeare makes it clear that the king has put this friendship totally behind him. The account of Falstaff's death—"The King has broke his heart"—belongs in this play. Both directors include it, though they both drop Fluellen's comparison of Henry with "Alexander the pig," who "killed his friend Cleitus" just as Harry Monmouth "turned away the fat knight" (IV.vi.16–55). Olivier also omits any mention of Bardolph's hanging and Henry's approval of the execution. Branagh includes it, but offers even more: he gives us what everyone has always wanted to know about Henry, and what Shakespeare—in any *stage* production—chooses *not* to tell us, namely, what the king is thinking and how he feels about his former friends.

In the scene in which Bardolph is hanged for stealing a pax, Branagh does this by moving the camera closer and closer and then revising Shakespeare. Although Henry V, in the three plays in which he appears, speaks more lines than any other character in Shakespeare's works, Shakespeare deliberately keeps us at a distance from him. He has only three soliloquies in the entire series. Most reviewers of Branagh's film have remarked on the camera's frequent and intense scrutinizing of Henry's face. These facial close-ups—which are not possible in the wooden O—aim to make up for the lack of self-conscious and revealing soliloquies by Shakespeare's enigmatic king. In the hanging of Bardolph, Branagh boldly takes the last step available in his film art: his camera takes us into the thoughts and memories of Henry. Olivier's film, for good political reasons, gives us a distant, rousing, heroic version of Henry V, who is depicted as both a competent political "actor" and a knight in shining armor. The brief Falstaff flashbacks in the earlier film serve as exposition or reminders for the audience, rather than attempts to convey what *Henry* is feeling. Branagh's more psychological approach results in a more sentimental version. Shakespeare's text gives no indication that the king is thinking about his former friends from Eastcheap. But Branagh's film satisfies our *hopes* that he is. Politics sometimes forces one to abandon and even to hurt one's friends. But even a calculating king does this with regret. Branagh means to "illustrate the young king's intense isolation and his difficulty in rejecting his former tavern life."[12] As at Harfleur, he does what he must, but he's suffering within. The close-ups of Branagh repeatedly reveal his tears. In Act Two, the betrayed lover's embrace in which Branagh holds the traitor at Southampton, shows his passionate care about friendship. In Act Three of Shakespeare's play, Pistol pleads with Fluellen to spare his friend Bardolph. But Shakespeare makes the brief moment almost comic, couching the plea for mercy in Pistol's usual overblown rhetoric:

> Let gallows gape for dog; let man go free
> And let not hemp his windpipe suffocate. (III.vi.44—45)

Branagh's film expands the incident into a major scene. The king arrives, recognizes Bardolph, and allows him to be executed as an example to the soldiers. But we witness the thoughts not visible to the soldiers. Here the camera can easily do something that is only done awkwardly in the live theater: it can depict events in the past. We are given a poignant flashback to the tavern, where Hal and his former companions shared food, ale, laughter, and friendship. In the film, Branagh places Falstaff's plea to Hal—"Do not when thou art king, hang a thief" (*1HIV,* I.ii.64)—in the mouth of Bardolph, and the king weeps to remember. The flashback is especially moving after Branagh's beautiful tavern scene in Act One. When it fades, the king "forces out"[13] his disinterested approval of the hanging of the thief: "We would have all offenders thus cut off" (III.vi.112). Branagh also emends Shakespeare, and increases our sympathy for Pistol and Bardolph, by making them, as well as Falstaff, old. The king's entire interview with the French herald, Montjoy, takes place under Bardolph's swinging corpse. In Shakespeare's play, Bardolph's execution is only *reported* to the king, and there is no indication that the fate of his former friend troubles him at all. Shakespeare's juxtaposition of Bardolph's death and the Montjoy interview may well suggest that the necessities of political rule leave little room for past attachments, and that King Henry is a very tough young man. Branagh's wrenching tears for his "old" companions are clearly an addition. If the king had to break Falsaff's heart and execute Bardolph, we should feel that these harsh necessities have broken his own heart, too. Most viewers remember this scene as one of the most moving parts of the film.

On the night before the battle of Agincourt, the unity of Henry's England is questioned in yet another way. In Henry's walk among his

troops and fireside talk with his common soldiers, Shakespeare suggests more seams in the smooth fabric of the organic community
Henry claims he is leading. A young soldier named Williams wonders
about the price of dying for the king's cause, and whether that cause
is just. The scene ends with a challenge to Henry. The poetic Chorus
of Act Four speaks of the comforting effect of "a little touch of Harry
in the night," but the prose of the ensuing dark scene is spoken by
soldiers who don't recognize the campfire visitor as their king, and
who are silenced, but hardly comforted, by the exchange. Here, as
often in the play, the Chorus gives the more romantic, idealized view
of Henry V, the one that he himself seems to have developed for his
subjects and their descendants. It is not surprising, therefore, that the
Chorus is retained with greater prominence in the Olivier version. In
the scenes that follow, Shakespeare repeatedly counterpoints the
Chorus's descriptions by depicting them more fully, and by including
ambiguous and worrisome behavior on the part of this "mirror of all
Christian kings." We have seen this with the clerics, and at both
Southampton and Harfleur, scenes, which Olivier had to edit heavily.
Before the battle of Agincourt, Olivier, who acts for democratic
audiences, characteristically emphasizes Henry's fellowship with the
common soldiers; it is the French who are the full-blown medieval
aristocrats.[14] Branagh, also in character, emphasizes the young king's
own doubts and fears. On the eve of the battle, the king of England is
also thinking about the differences between private citizens and those
who determine the destiny of nations. Branagh also restores the lines
about the murder of Richard II, which Olivier cuts from the prayer to
the "God of battles." Young Henry is worried, even desperate, on the
night before the battle.

Only when day returns does the "warlike Harry, like himself" knit
his heterogeneous and ragtag army into the single force that faces the
French later that day. Once again, Henry is "a prince to act" and his
triumph is achieved through his last great speech on Crispin's day,
before the decisive battle. Like "Once more unto the breach," this
speech aims to unify Irish-English-Scots-Welsh Englishmen, and to
turn nobles, yeomen, and riffraff into a "nation," "a band of brothers," tied to each other forever, if not by nature, then by their bravery
on the field of Agincourt. In it Henry offers a modern speech that
again makes us reflect on the one his grandfather had given (in *Richard
II*) about the "scept'red isle." Gaunt's speech emphasizes the natural
and the organic: geographical integrity, "this little world," "this happy
breed of men," and defense of home. World renown is the result of

"true chivalry" in a supernational cause; no other nation is mentioned, nor are any individuals. Henry's speech, in contrast, is about the consolidation, under one particular leader, of a political and military community by means of heroic deeds far away from home. The speech is built upon names.

In "Once more unto the breach," the king first addresses the gentry—"on, on, you noble English"—exhorting them to set an example "to men of grosser blood." The former remind him of Alexander, a universal model for men of fighting spirit. The latter are homegrown, "good yeomen," "whose limbs were made in England," reared in English pasture, as if organically attached to and nurtured by the land in which they are born. They, too, are "worthy of their breeding," "noble," at least in spirit. At Agincourt, Henry again appeals to the organic ties between noble aristocrats and sturdy yeomen. He evokes a scene of future Englishmen remembering the deeds of the "happy few" who fought upon the feast of Crispian. He begins by mentioning the names of the nobles and moves to a confirmation that the "band of brothers" includes *all* who "fought with us upon St. Crispin's day" (IV.iii.67). The holiday in honor of the brother cobblers, saints of lowly origins, once united those who celebrated it as brothers in Christ's blood. Henry is done, the Christian holy day has been transformed into a patriotic English holiday. Future Englishmen will remember their forbears as those who were not by blood a "happy breed," but who were transformed into "brothers" by Henry's speech and by shedding their blood with Henry V. As France becomes England, the French field of Agincourt is transformed into the location of an English victory.

The differences between the two films at this famous passage are interesting, especially since both are beautiful to see and moving to hear. Olivier, characteristically, starts among his men, who gather around him. The camera follows him closely up a bridge and then moves back at eye level—he is no longer the underdog, as he appears in "Once more." but is in full command.[15] As the great speech expands in subject and in volume, the camera moves back to include all the men and then the whole camp. Interestingly, we don't focus on those we've come to know as individuals in the earlier acts. All attention is on Henry, who binds his men to each other and to himself entirely by means of his speech, the greatest political instrument he has. The clerics were right in Act One when they emphasized his ability to talk. Olivier delivers the great speech a cappella; the music begins only after he has vaulted onto his horse, and the camera has turned to the preparation of the bows.

Branagh's Crispin speech is equally moving, but differs, once again, in emphasizing the psychological and personal over the political achievement of Henry's speech. The camera moves back to group the soldiers into a "band of brothers" bound together by Henry. But it also moves among the troops, lingering on Nym, Williams, the boy, and Erpingham, each of whom we've come to care about, and about whom Branagh's film convinces us that Henry is still thinking. This is touching and satisfying, but, again, it results in a sentimentalizing or softening of the play. Branagh's continuous orchestration through the entire speech is heard by the film's audience, but not, of course, by the soldiers at Agincourt. Canterbury had told Ely that in Henry's "discourse of war," one could hear "a fearful battle rend'red you in music" (I.i.44). Branagh's real music throughout the speech intensifies the effect, but perhaps it diminishes our sense that Henry does it all through talk and the force of his own calculating personality.

When comparing "Once more unto the breach" and the Agincourt speeches as they are done in the two films, it is instructive to keep in mind the directors' motives for making their films. Whatever his artistic aims may have been, Olivier's primary motive, as we have seen, was unashamedly political. Before he undertook the full-length film, he himself had experienced the effect of the two great speeches—he calls them "arias"—on British soldiers who heard them in the camp entertainments he had staged earlier in the war. In *On Acting,* he describes how with the Crispin speech he "was able to whip up my wartime audience of real soldiers, urging them forward with me":[16]

By the time I got to "God for Harry" they would have followed me anywhere. Looking back, I don't think we could have won the war without "Once more unto the breach . . ." somewhere in our soldier's hearts.[17]

His Henry is a "showman, an organizer, a public man . . . an almost entirely externalized image of a hero,"[18] a leader to fire the hearts of the underdog English as they valiantly attempted to hold out against the Nazi enemy. Branagh obviously has a less-political interest. He is more concerned to convey to his peacetime audience the

qualities of introspection, fear, doubt and anger which I believed the text indicated: an especially young Henry with more than a little Hamlet in

him. It was conveying these elements of the king's personality that gave
me the initial idea for a new screen version—the idea of abandoning large-
theater projection and allowing close-ups and low-level dialogue to draw
the audience into the *human side* of this distant medieval world [empha-
sis added].[19]

The interest in the personal and psychological would naturally shift the
emphasis from the grand arias to low-level dialogue. We are meant to
understand and sympathize with Henry, not simply to follow him—or
his descendants—into battle. You can't do *Henry V* without the great
speeches. But Branagh uses the close camera and avoids declamatory
acting as much as he can in order to shift the audience's attention
to the king's insides. For him the "human side" often means the
private side.

Let us, at last, turn to the battle, to the scenes that Shakespeare's
Chorus says the wooden O cannot adequately represent. What can the
silver screen offer? The unlikely English victory at Agincourt is
something of a mystery. The history books will tell you that the feudal
French, tied to their old chivalric ways, were defeated because the
smaller army of English yeoman efficiently used an effective modern
weapon, the longbow. Unencumbered by heavy armor, any commoner
could, from afar, disable more enemy soldiers than could a noble on
horseback or a foot soldier with a dagger in close individual combat.
Olivier, the actor who knows Henry is an actor, has it both ways, for
the movies can supply the battle that was beyond the capacity of the
wooden O. He gives us speeches *and* the colorful military differences
between the French and English, turning the French dauphin into a
feeble coward, absorbed by his own fatuous talk of glory and, especially, of his horse. Olivier adds the archers; the release of their arrows
is one of the most memorable moments in the film. But the point about
the French horses is Shakespeare's. Olivier emphasizes it visually in
the shots of the French horses reflected in puddles and in the memorable contrast between Henry's easy leap onto his horse and the armored
dauphin, who is escorted by an obsequious, bowing servant, and who
finally has to be lowered onto his horse with a pulley. There is also a
long French cavalry charge to music. But the long-awaited battle really
begins as the king drops his hand in signal to the archers. The
breathtaking first flight of the English arrows is followed by footage of
the French horses running toward the English stakes, and by shots of
English yeoman dropping from the trees like Robin Hoods onto the
French knights on horseback below. Throughout Olivier's battle, the

French and English are distinguishable by differences in their costumes and colors, as well as by the way they fight. They keep rallying around their leaders who prominently display flags.

Olivier's battle is bright and sunny; as one disparaging reviewer comments, "The famous victories of a fairy-tale prince should be bloodless, beautiful, and in Technicolor."[20] The only blood in the film is seen on the English luggage boy whose throat is cut by the French. Fluellen, weeping, rightly insists, "Tis expressly again the law of arms," and Gower reports that, in anger at the French, Henry has "caused every soldier to cut his prisoner's throat" (IV.vii.9–10). Some of Shakespeare's readers might remember the barbarous Welsh treatment of war prisoners as it was reported way back at the beginning of *Henry IV, Part One.* And some of Olivier's viewers might be reminded of Nazi war atrocities in their own time.[21] Now, in Shakespeare's text, the order to kill the prisoners comes *before* Henry has learned about the boys, and is provoked only by the news that the French have "reinforced their scattered men" (IV.vi.36–37). It seems that the "mirror of all Christian kings" will do anything to win this battle. But neither Olivier's nor Branagh's Henry gives the order then. Their two Henrys differ, but both directors apparently find Shakespeare's Henry too calculating and too ruthless for their taste, too willing himself to disregard the conventional "laws of arms" and to follow merely the "law of nature." Both cut the order about the prisoners of war and emphasize the French inhumanity to the boys. Olivier rides out in righteous anger to avenge their slaughter in a heroic single combat with the French constable. Once again, Olivier has it both ways: yeoman longbows and a royal duel in shining armor. A circle of spectators forms around the two chivalric opponents and cheers when the knight on the white horse—now an *English* knight—defeats the black-clad bad guy on the black horse. From beginning to end, the king has directed the battle. The French herald returns to Henry and acknowledges defeat by kneeling before him; victor and vanquished are clearly distinguished. The two armies depart separately from the field, the French retreating quickly on horses, and the English in a slow, winding recessional across the countryside to the hymn "Non Nobis." In most of these scenes, the camera has the English point of view and, thus, so does the film's audience.

Branagh's battle, in contrast to Olivier's, is full of the blood and mud of real war, but the slow-motion photography, again with continuous musical accompaniment, makes the sequence almost surreal. The slow-motion camera can do for time what the zooming camera does for space, namely exaggerate or de-emphasize what the natural human being would experience. In his published introduction to the film script, Branagh says it was essential to limit the film to two hours: hence, his many cuts from the play. But he chooses to slow down, and thus to lengthen, parts of the battle portion of the film, with the effect of emphasizing the horror and nightmarish feel—to any *one* participant on *either* side. Throughout the earlier acts, Branagh has avoided turning the French into caricatures, as Olivier does. The dauphin is vain and unpleasant, the king is worried and ill, but we are not given a wholesale reduction as we are in the earlier film. Instead of viewing the fighting from a distance and thus distinguishing political sides, as Olivier does, Branagh's camera singles out individuals from both sides: Montjoy, the constable, the dauphin, Bates, Williams, York, and, most memorably, Nym and Pistol. Even in the midst of the battle, these two are cutting purses from the corpses. In an earlier scene that both directors cut, the boy calls them "sworn brothers in filching" (III.ii.45–46). In the confused havoc of battle, the "law of nature" prevails and the focus is on the self. But our proper disgust at their incurable selfishness is muted when Nym is stabbed and Pistol embraces him. Branagh says that we see the "old man's [Pistol's] anguish at the loss of his companion."[22] As for the band of brothers, at best, the bonds of private friendship are more evident than broader political bonds. Effective political rhetoric, like Henry's Crispin speech, must work hard to counter this law of nature. At the end of the Crispin speech, Branagh raises his clenched hand and the soldiers respond together with the same gesture. But once the battle begins, every hand is for itself.

But Branagh's battle goes even farther. During the opening charge of the French cavalry—we hear the galloping getting closer and closer—the camera again singles out the familiar faces of individuals. Each terrified soldier faces the enemy alone. After moving from political sides to individuals, the camera moves in so close to the participants that we see only fragments, and hear only muffled sounds or an isolated clang of weapons. Part montage, part movie, part slow-motion movie, Branagh's battle is an animated Guernica, with falling horses, a human head bleeding at the mouth, and "all those legs and arms, and heads chopped off in battle" that Williams had weighed against the king's cause the night before the battle (IV.i.137–38). Falstaff, too, had worried that not even personal honor, much less that of one's country, was worth an arm or a leg (*1HV,* V.i.127–41). The parts of the body point to the sameness of all human beings. Though their rulers, customs, holidays, and languages may differ, what they have in common is anatomy. But the parts of one's own body cannot be common. Dying for one's nation or king means elevating a public cause above personal survival, the law of nations above the law of nature. It requires looking away from "all those legs and arms." Branagh wants us to look hard at them, and he even slows or stops his camera to make sure that we see. He would agree with the reviewer cited above: war is full of blood, and is ugly, all the more so in Technicolor.[23]

Though Branagh's film is hardly the pacifist version some viewers expected, it does tend to qualify Henry's victory by emphasizing the bewildering horror of war. Branagh's Henry is a courageous, effective commander, but he is no knight in shining armor; unlike Olivier, he wears only brown wool and chain mail. Down-to-earth, he dismounts and fights on the ground among his men; it is not clear that he, or any leader, directs the fighting after it has begun. At the end, when the herald asks permission to collect his dead, the exhausted English king confesses, "I tell thee truly, herald, I know not if the day be ours or no" (IV.vii.86). His bewilderment is a bit of a distortion on Branagh's part since in Shakespeare's play Henry says that he doesn't know whether England is victorious because he still sees French soldiers galloping around the battlefield. Olivier cuts the line completely; his sunlit victory is visible to everyone. Branagh's victory takes place in rain; when Branagh is told of the French defeat, he stumbles and falls just as he did after Harfleur surrendered. His victories are always qualified by falls. In the aftermath of the battle, Branagh has us watch the *victors* carry their dead and wounded from the field. The brotherhood of all human beings is seen in their exhaustion and in their vulnerable dead bodies.

At the end, Pistol and dead Nym, dauphin and dead constable are equally objects of our pity in a way that they are not in Olivier's triumphant victory. The saddest of all is the murdered luggage boy; in Branagh's film he is recognizably *Falstaff's* boy. Though Shakespeare has him vow to leave Pistol and Nym earlier in the play (III.ii) and never mentions him again, Branagh keeps him before us throughout the fighting. Henry carries his body across the corpse-strewn field in the long recessional after the battle. Once again, we see that the king is still somehow attached to the Boar's Head companions of his more carefree youth. As he places the boy on the cart with the bodies of other dead children, Henry kisses him. The film script says that his "bloodstained and exhausted face" shows the "dreadful price they have all had to pay for this *so-called* victory. . . . His head drops as if in shame [emphasis added]."[24]

As for an explanation of the victory, the longbows are never mentioned by *Shakespeare*. He makes it seem as though the victory *was* a miracle, that God really *was* for "Harry, England and St. George." Or should we say that Shakespeare's *Henry* makes it seem that way? The real miracle, as we have seen, was in Henry's ability to act and to speak to inspire the English to fight as they did that day. One might say that Agincourt, like Harfleur, is taken by a speech. Perhaps this is why *Shakespeare* does not mention the longbows or follow the Crispin speech with any attempt to represent the battle itself. The son of the king who spoke of Crusades until his dying day, now orders "Non Nobis" and "Te Deum" to be sung: "Praised be God, and not our strength for it" (IV.vii.89). It is useful if one's victory—as well as one's reformation—is thought to be a miracle. Like Machiavelli, Shakespeare suggests that the king should appear religious, but be willing, if necessary, to speak the way Henry does before Harfleur. Shakespeare's Henry seems aware that he is manipulating thought. But oddly, our two modern Henrys—both knight-in-shining-armor and exhausted boy-ruler—seem almost to believe in the miracle. So might their twentieth-century audiences, moved by the tremendous swells of twentieth-century movie music that accompany the recessionals after the battle, especially in Branagh's film, where the first voice chanting the beautiful hymn is joined by more and more voices and, finally, by a full orchestra.

Part Three:
England and France (Act Five)

Henry V does not end with the decisive battle. All of Act Five is to follow. The Chorus once more reminds us of the limitations of a staged play. The films have no such limitations. Branagh's film omits the Chorus and the fight between Pistol and Fluellen, which he finds dull and "unfunny,"[25] and moves directly from the "Non Nobis" hymn to the treaty negotiations in the French palace. Olivier gives us one final scene with Fluellen in France, as he humiliates Pistol for his earlier insults about the Welsh leek. In Act Three, Scene Two, Shakespeare intends Bardolph's cries of "To the breach" to qualify Henry's heroic exhortation "once more unto the breach" in the previous scene. In his last appearance, Pistol, one of the "sworn brothers in filching," vows to fake his wounds and swear "he got them in the Gallia wars," ironically echoing Henry's Crispin day speech to the "band of brothers." In Olivier's earlier scene, one can hardly hear Bardolph and his companions, and the irony of what they are shouting is lost. In this last scene, too, the setting—a winter scene from a French medieval manuscript—is so pretty, and Fluellen so cute and Pistol so stagey that the ironic echoes of Henry's high-flown, heroic rhetoric are hardly noticed. Olivier turns ambiguous material that, even as we laugh at it, might raise uncomfortable questions about Henry's enterprise and the fragile unity of his nation, into mere good-humored stage business. And he turns Pistol's humiliation by Fluellen into a warm-hearted endorsement of the "Englishness" of all the heterogeneous elements in Henry's nation.

Shakespeare's next scene returns to serious business. Both directors are certainly interested in the union of England and France into one nation. Even if, as has been suggested, there is no natural determination of a country, and even if a nation is merely a construct of the able man who governs it and extends it by acquisition, it is prudent for that man to attempt some natural union of the parts that are assimilated. In the last act of the play, both French and English again begin calling each other "brother," "cousin," and "son," accepting and asserting natural ties between the two royal families. The successful conquest of France requires that the Frenchmen, too, be included in the band of brothers that Henry calls "England." The marriage of Henry and Katherine promises to produce an heir naturally descended from both England and France, just as Henry himself is usefully both English and Welsh. Unlike Mortimer, who cannot speak to his Welsh wife even after they are married, Henry can learn to get along with anyone in any language. As he tells his friend Poins, in *Henry IV, Part One*, "I can drink with any tinker in his own language" (*1HIV*, II.iv.19), and "I am sworn brother to a leash of drawers, and can call them all by their Christen names, as Tom, Dick, and Francis" (*1HIV*, II.iv.6–8). He might have said "Harry!" Now, as King Henry V, he woos Katherine in his broken French, and assures her that "fashions" and "nice customs cursy to great kings" (V.ii.281); they will kiss regardless of local conventions. This is charming in both films. But *Shakespeare's* play also shows us that Henry disregards even international conventions by threatening to rape and butcher the civilians of Harfleur and by ordering his "noble English" to cut the throats of enemy prisoners. Likewise, he justifies his invasion of France by getting his clergy to interpret not only Salique, but also biblical, law, simply in accordance with his will. Conventional language only looks like a natural definer of nations. Nations, like marriages, may appear to be made in heaven or by nature, but they are often the creations of down-to-earth men who have the speech and strength to take what they want. That this history play ends like a comedy—in marriage—is a sign of the difference between Henry *V* and his predecessors on the throne. Shakespeare's Machiavellian prince, like Machiavelli's comic hero/prince is applauded by the audience at the happy ending.[26]

The language lesson in Act Three, Scene Four shows Katherine to be as apt a student of languages—and of political necessity—as her future husband is. She says "it is necessary" ("il faut que") that she learn to speak as "les natifs d'Angleterre" do, that is, to call the body parts she shares by nature with all human beings by the conventional names attached to them in England. Just as new borders and names may be imposed on the physical contours of the lands men govern, so new names—even ones that sound like words which "dames d'honneur" of one nation would never utter—may "nevertheless" be used for the parts of the body. Henry V is not defined or confined by the language, customs, or borders of his nation. Rather, he is the maker of these conventions, and he will impose them on others. His freedom and flexibility are indicated in his language shifts and in his easy use of different versions of his own name. In Act Five, Scene Two, when the the English conqueror and his French princess meet, he appropriately anglicizes her name; Katherine becomes "Kate" to his "Harry."

The Katherine scenes in both films are charming. The differences between them are consistent with other differences noted throughout. In Branagh's version, the fun of the language lesson ends abruptly when Katherine opens the door and glimpses her somber father, along with the Constable, dauphin, and other lords, heading for the council chamber to prepare for the immanent war. We can sympathize with both French and English. In Olivier, the scene comes to an end undisturbed in this way. It is preceded and followed by distant views of the French nobles in the courtyard below. Like all the French scenes in the earlier film it is set in the medieval fairy-tale settings that Olivier modeled on calendar imitations of the illuminations in *Les Trés Riches Heures* of the Duc du Berri. All is beautiful, symmetrical, carefully colored, and in place. Even in a realistic movie, it feels static and artificial. This was, perhaps, the way the world might sometimes have looked to the divine-right king, Richard II. The Lancastrian usurpation brought an end to this supposedly unchanging medieval order that was thought somehow to be guaranteed by God. Olivier's

Henry bursts in upon the certainty and symmetry of this pretty but feeble French picture-book world, imposing his own order on it, just as his father had burst in upon and reconstructed Richard's kingdom. But, again, Olivier manages to have it both ways. His Henry woos Katherine in awkward bent positions suggesting the "invasion of the pictorial composition which typifies the spatial disposition in the French palace."[27] But the filmed play ends with a happily-ever-after fairy-tale marriage. As in all such stories, we simply assume that the prince loves the princess and we don't think much about it. The courtship ends in a mutual kiss. The camera then moves back to include the applauding French and English representatives, who have completed their peace negotiations. The French king blesses the happy couple and joins their hands before the now-united court. At this point, Olivier reverses his usual practice of moving the camera back to include the assembled company in the scene. Here he zooms in to fill the screen with a close-up shot of the royal couple's clasped hands; we might be reminded of Katherine's first English word. Unlike the body parts in Branagh's battle, these hands are public. The unusual close-up shows the signet rings of the two nations. The joined hands signify a political as well as private union.

Branagh's more realistic courtship scenes—his Katherine is less delicate looking than Olivier's and the settings are less picturesque— make us feel that, at last, Henry's public and personal needs coincide. After all those tearful sacrifices, we believe him when he kisses her and says he loves her. We want to, just as we wanted to believe that he suffered over Bardolph's execution and Falstaff's boy. Like Olivier's, Branagh's film omits Henry's earlier refusal of the French king's offer of Katherine and some petty dukedoms (III.Chorus.29–31). He also cuts the last negotiations with the French, which remind us that France *must* agree to England's terms. Gone also are the lines about the forced entry of cities' "maiden walls" (V.ii.30–35), which in Shakespeare's text are reminiscent of Henry's terrible speech at Harfleur.

Olivier leaves us feeling good: about Henry V, about his conquest of France, about his marriage, and about his prospects for an heir. This was his intention in making this film for England in 1944. The return to the Globe Theater and Elizabethan London at the end of the film reminds us, as Shakespeare's plays do, that Henry the politician was a consummate actor. It concludes Olivier's contrast between the capacities of staged and filmed plays to transport us to other times and places. At the end, we are returned to the Globe Theater and reminded that the princess is really a boy actor, and that the courtiers' medieval clothing is really Elizabethan stage costume. The playhouse flag goes down, and we get a last glimpse of London Tower, still standing strong.[28] The film's original English audience is reminded that they, and the armed services mentioned in the credits, and Churchill, and the whole world of civilized nations, are fighting to preserve the nation that produced, among other things, Shakespeare and the Globe Theater. It would be hard, at the end of this film, not to wish yourself English and part of a very special band of brothers. Olivier quite understandably omits the last speech of the Chorus, who, in Shakespeare, reappears to tell us that the son of this fairy-tale couple lost all that his dashing father had attained.

Branagh, as one would expect, does not leave us with the English victory and fairy-tale marriage as our last impressions. His film insists that, though you can get closer to the king, you can't turn a history play into a comedy. He restores the Epilogue, suggesting to the end that war is terrible, that the failures and victories of even great leaders are the results of Fortune as well as of God's will and their own, and that no 'miracle' lasts forever. In contrast to the identifiably English Chorus in the earlier film, the cosmopolitan, arty, black-clad film director who speaks the Epilogue, makes us feel detached rather than patriotic. The film leaves us drained and sobered by the carnage and sacrifices human beings endure for the sake of "politics." Since World War II, we have become both more private and more cosmopolitan, and the middle realm of patriotic attachment to an extended but exclusive nation has become more problematic for us. Branagh's film is for our time in this way: he consistently emphasizes the personal and the private, and, thus, the universal and shared concerns of his characters. What he calls the human side tends toward the subnational or the supranational. The middle realm, which is most properly political, is less on his mind.[29]

Part Four:
Public Entertainment: The Wooden O and the Movies

After the remarkable though different virtues of these two films, one might ask whether the stage play that Shakespeare wrote can ever return to the wooden O and still hold our attention there. Indeed, since Olivier's film appeared, many productions of the play have self-consciously attempted to reproduce on stage what he did with the camera.[30] No doubt Branagh's version will have a similar influence over the coming years. But can the theater do anything that the movies cannot do?

Despite the Chorus's apologies and regrets about the inadequacies of a staged play, there may be a price to be paid for the technical powers of the filmed one. The camera can show not only large numbers of people and different places, but also clothing, objects, furniture, the outdoors, and the weather out there, in full realistic detail. This means, in effect, less awareness in the viewer that the people, clothing, objects, rooms, and noises before him are actors, costumes, props, scenery, and sound effects. Representation becomes presentation as we forget that we are watching an imitation. This has the further effect of reducing our distance from what we are watching. The more we are immersed in the "immediate sensation of sound and light" and the realistic experience of the actors, the less active may be our critical judgment of what we are watching.[31] Even music, the shifting placement of the camera, and slow-motion sequences do not undermine our increased sense that the scene before us is real. The realistic *spectacle* of the film surely distracts even the best listener from the *language* of the play. Our attention can't help but be divided, even though we may be less likely to miss lines or mis-hear at the movies.

Furthermore, the staged play, with its acknowledged theatrical conventions, is the proper place for heightened prose or poetic language. An original film script in *poetry* is a rare phenomenon. Although films have been made of the poetic plays of Shakespeare and of other writers, most movies are prosaic. Their linguistic naturalism matches their visual naturalism. They have memorable scenes and lines, but they very rarely have memorable speeches. They also lack the convention that Shakespeare and other poetic playwrights use, of shifting between poetry and prose, or among different kinds of verse. In any good film script, different people speak differently and the same person may speak differently at different times. But it is precisely the acknowledged artificiality of theater speech that allows for greater flexibility on stage than on film. The history plays, which are, among other things, about speech and acting, are remarkable for the variety and richness of their language. Olivier and Branagh have Shakespeare's rich text and deliver it beautifully in the filmed versions of the play. The question is whether we *hear* it in the same way in the films. For example, is the importance of the Crispin day speech diminished, and do we pay less attention to Henry's extraordinary language when the speech is followed by the long spectacular battle sequence that Shakespeare never could have presented—and perhaps never *wanted* to present—on stage? Again, in the theater, there may be music, but it rarely *accompanies* speech. Furthermore, we can see its *source*, as we do in Olivier's Globe. In the movies, the full orchestration of invisible music, even under the most elaborate speech, has manipulative power far beyond that of intermittent theater music. Is this always an advantage?

Perhaps we should consider briefly plays that are filmed, not for movie theaters, but expressly for television viewing. Productions like the BBC Shakespeare plays may offer the realism of films without the danger of wide-screen spectacles distracting from the language.[32] But one often finds that the very close-ups that can render televised speech so clearly, make the dialogue appear more private than public, by framing one or a few actors, rather than the whole ensemble. The spectator of a staged production cannot "focus" so exclusively on one speaker, but must always be aware, at least peripherally, of the group. Television and films tend to do what Branagh does: to use this powerful ability of the camera to reveal personal psychology in close-ups, flashbacks, and voice-over soliloquies, sometimes at the expense of the group or political scene.

In the ancient theater, the public point of view of the spectators was maintained by the convention of the *skēnē*, a stage-set that represents the outside facade of a building, such as the palace of Atreus or the public court in Athens. Action within was reported to the audience by those who emerged from within. The modern stage convention of removing the fourth wall allows audiences a privileged view of what is going on inside. It is no accident that plays presented in such theaters became more and more concerned with private subjects, like family and internal psychology. The continued presence of the proscenium stage, however, keeps the theater audience aware that it is watching a play. The movies go one step further. By eliminating the frame of the stage, they allow the audience to look, without even a reminder that a fourth wall has been removed. The result, as we have seen, is the greatly increased ability to convey internal thoughts, as well as internal scenes. Many have worried about the increased risks of voyeurism as well.

The contrast between the public emphasis of staged plays and the private emphasis of filmed plays might also be considered with respect to what surrounds the play itself—the context around the text, the *activity* of play or movie watching. Olivier's film, which begins and ends as a staged play, gives as sunny and idealized a view of playgoing in Elizabethan London as it does of King Henry V. Nevertheless, it suggests some important differences between seeing *Henry V* in the wooden O and seeing it at the movies. Olivier depicts the play as a public event. Playbills, the raised flag, and a trumpet fanfare draw citizens from all walks of life to a place set aside for watching. Most of them would have walked or come in open boats across the river; their coming is a visible, public event. The location of the Globe Theater and its peculiar status as a recognized public institution, marginal but regulated, is a fascinating subject. What interests me here is that going to the Globe means going out into the city—actually slightly outside the city—in broad daylight, and recognizing familiar private homes and public landmarks, one of which is the theater itself. Although the Elizabethan theaters were private commercial ventures, they were, for the most part, highly visible, freestanding buildings with the status of public monuments.[33] In Visscher's view of London, for example, the Globe and the Bear Garden face St. Paul's across the river, and are identified as noteworthy landmarks. Olivier's Elizabethan playgoers greet their fellow citizens and watch actors who are, apparently, already familiar to them. The audience is visibly articulated by its behavior, clothing, and seating. Some patrons have paid more than others for their tickets, and some, seated on the stage, are more on display than others.[34] Although there is no official acknowledgment or civic ceremony as there was in ancient Athens, this theater, too, is a place where one comes to see and to be seen: by one's fellow citizens, and by foreign visitors and ambassadors.[35] Contemporary reports indicate that there were plenty of spies looking around as well.

Also, as in Athens, the daytime performance and the roundness of the wooden O insure that, even after they are absorbed in the play, the spectators remain, in some way, aware of themselves and of each other. The Chorus's addresses to the acknowledged audience have the same effect. At the conclusion of the performance, some spectators eagerly come on stage to congratulate the Chorus and company. The handclapping and handshakes are a sign of the communal nature of this public entertainment. Like the hands of Princess Katherine and King Henry in Olivier's film, they are the hands of individuals joined in a wider community. Like the spectators in the theater of Dionysus, the English audience that watches a *stage* production of *Henry V* on May 1, 1600, retains some sense of *itself* as a whole. Furthermore, the Elizabethan stage

> was the only major medium for social intercommunication, the only existing form of journalism and the only occasion for the gathering of large numbers of people other than for sermons and for executions.[36]

Its *unofficial* civic function was thus, in another way, even more prominent than that of the theater in Athens. It was certainly regulated, a sign of how seriously it was taken by the public authorities. Regulation that consists primarily of restrictions to prevent disorder, sedition, and plague differs greatly from regulation that requires arrangements aimed at the positive civic education of the citizens; this difference in regulation is characteristic of the difference between the modern commercial state and the ancient city.

As the city has grown larger, more heterogeneous, and more cosmopolitan, our theatergoing has become a less-public activity. Since much of the population rarely, if ever, chooses to attend a live play, and since different parts of the population are attracted to different kinds of "shows," there really isn't a clearly defined citizen audience. Our theaters are more likely to be housed in art "complexes" than in freestanding monuments, and we are more likely to arrive in private cars at night, than by foot in broad daylight. We rarely meet friends or neighbors in the audience, and have no contact with the actors. Nevertheless, the live theater remains, to some extent, a place to observe and be observed by others. There is still a special public air of excitement and anticipation as people stream into Lincoln Center or the Barbican before a performance. The walk across the bridge to the South Bank Centre in London preserves, perhaps, something of what it might have felt like four hundred years ago to arrive at the Globe via the Thames, with the river, city, and one's fellow theatergoers in full view. Inside the theater, even in large democratic cities, the audience is still articulated into parts. The people in the orchestra and boxes—no one gets to sit on stage anymore—may look different from those in the upper balcony; they have paid different prices to watch the same show. The lobbies and refreshment bars serving different sections may also reflect these different prices.[37] Although the lights go down as the play begins, even in a rectangular theater with the specators all facing forward, it is not unusual to notice those around you; somehow they, too, still "show." In a live production, the mood and reactions of the audience surely influence each viewer's responses. Stage conventions, the limitations of the wooden O, and intermissions in which the lights go up remind you constantly that the absorbing action before you is a contained imitation, and that you are still sitting in the real world.

What about the movies? When Olivier decided to film *Henry V* in 1944, he had in mind to expose large numbers of English people to the speeches and whole play he'd been presenting live in military camps and London theaters. He did everything he could to allude to and to keep viewers conscious of their own position and identity, and to manipulate their responses to his artfully simplified version of a very complex play. The making of this film was a public event. It was sponsored by the very polity it aimed to serve, and its viewers were reminded of this at the beginning and end.

Despite the use of films for public purposes—there are other notable British movies from the time of World War Two—the increasing predominance of the movies as a form of entertainment indicates the increased privacy of our lives. Paradoxically, they are a *public* form of entertainment that , more than the live theater, arranges for *isolated* watching. The same film is shown in many places at the same—or different—times. The audiences that see it do so less as a community and more at their own individual convenience. All pay the same price for tickets and have little interest in their neighbors or in the unarticulated audience that surrounds them. They sit in parallel rows, in complete darkness, concentrating their full attention on magnified actors on a huge, brightly lit screen. Everyone knows the delightful feeling of going to a movie all alone, of thoroughly "losing oneself"— and one's real life—in the movie, and of emerging, several uninterrupted hours later, as if one has really been away. For the really serious connoisseurs of film, there are theaters where perfect darkness is assured, and the seats are not attached to each other. And nobody but children and the most unsophisticated still clap hands at the end of a movie; usually, there is no communal response.[38] The unpolitical character of moviegoing has become even more pronounced in the last few decades. No longer does a town's whole population eagerly await the arrival of an anticipated film in one big theater that had, especially for the young, the status of a community center. In cities, movies are no longer shown in enormous decorated "palaces," and suburban and rural theaters rarely distinguish themselves with some local motif or decor. Nowadays, there is enormous choice, as many films are shown simultaneously in identical tiny theaters in movie "complexes" in thousands of commercial suburban and urban shopping malls where one may feel more like a consumer than a spectator. You buy socks and books, toys and furniture, and a movie ticket, all at the same convenient place. You pay your money and you take your choice. Unlike the Athenian or Elizabethan plays that were watched by the whole population or by a cross-section of the whole, today's films, like today's plays, now cater to different audiences. *Cinema Paradiso* [39] is a phenomenon of the past.

Finally, between Olivier and Branagh we have acquired a technology undreamed of, not only by Shakespeare in his wooden O, but also by Olivier in his film studio. Today, the VCR, attached to anyone's TV, enables millions of private citizens of the world to watch Olivier in their living rooms, or Branagh from their beds. One can now see the play without going out in public at all. This *completely* private, placeless, timeless viewing, with no public context, can take place on private demand. Shakespeare's play and Olivier's film were public events connected to their times, noted by those who saw them and spoke of them to others. Branagh's film, despite its less-political aims, also originally appeared in a public context. Its first audiences waited on lines outside the theaters in which it was shown, and American reviewers compared it to *Glory* and *Born on the Fourth of July,* which were released at the same time. But now, the astonishing technology that allows me to watch both films again and again, to stop them at my convenience, and to compare their versions of this rich story, has, in some way, removed them from the public domain. From now on, most of the people who see Branagh's film—and Olivier's too, for that matter—will see them at home in familiar surroundings, with the lights on, often with interruptions for dessert and from the phone, visitors, children, and pets. The TV screen is part of the furniture, and the actors viewed on it are much smaller than the home-spectators, a striking difference from the magnified images we behold at the movies. When it is over, the film viewed on the VCR is hardly articulated from the life around it—by applause, house lights, or, often, even a change in position. And one can move from *Henry V* to *Saturday Night Live* with no transition. Because the films are always available at uniform low prices, many more people will see them than could previously.[40] These *Henry V* movies will continue to move viewers as they have before. But this "mass" audience, in some way, is no longer an audience, for its members watch privately and alone. The first thing one now sees on the Olivier *video* is a warning that "Any public performance is prohibited"; it is only for "private exhibition in homes."[41]

A long time ago, a Greek city required its citizens to attend public festivals in which the central activity was play-watching in a huge stone amphitheater. Nowadays, one can stretch out at home with *Gone wth the Wind, Rashomon,* or *Henry V,* and another film for every night of the week. Between the stone amphitheater and the comforts of home, is the wooden O—a "cockpit" full of "flat, unraisèd, spirits" who attempt through powerful language and the "imperfections" of their art to transport their audience to another time and place. Even as they were transported, however, the members of the Elizabethan English audience, like the members of the ancient Athenian audience, remained themselves; in this public place they were somehow at home. Their mixed way of viewing has now been largely superseded by the very power of the movie camera to transport movie-viewers more perfectly, even in the privacy of their own homes. And this new media technology has had an enormous effect on the political and social community that surrounds it. Restricting ourselves to *filmed* dramas—either at the movies or at home—would be a great loss. These two fine films are remarkable achievements, but one would hope—for the sake of preserving the complexity and the public character of the play—that Shakespeare's *Henry V* will also continue to be seen in the wooden O for which it was written.

Notes

1. Anthony Davies, *Filming Shakespeare's Plays: The Adaptations of Olivier, Wells, Brook, Kurosawa* (Cambridge, Mass., 1988), p. 30.

2. Harry M. Geduld, *Filmguide to Henry V* (Bloomington, Ind., 1973), p. 27. This is the most thorough account and analysis of the film that I know.

3. Graham Holderness says that Olivier's Globe Theater settings at the beginning of the film suggest that "this is a king who seems to rule more by the accomplished deployment of theatrical techniques than by statesmanship or good government (*Shakespeare Recycled: The Making of Historical Drama* [Hertfordshire, 1992], p. 187). In what follows I shall argue that "theatrical technique" is not an alternative to statesmanship, but a legitimate and necessary part of it.

4. Kenneth Branagh, *Henry V by William Shakespeare: A Screen Adaptation* (London, 1989), p. 12. This volume contains the complete transcript and many photos from the film. The director's brief introduction and stage directions are revealing.

5. Branagh, p. 47.

6. Geduld, pp. 37–43.

7. Branagh, p. 60.

8. Holderness underlines the marginal character of the Channel coast, and discusses the importance of the Channel cliffs in British "myths of origin," reminding us also that Olivier's wartime audiences were listening to Vera Lynn's emotionally charged home-front songs ("There'll be blue birds over the white cliffs of Dover") as well as to Olivier's Shakespearean orations (Holderness, pp. 194–210). Geography books, less sentimental than wartime songs, will remind you that the cliffs, and thus England's boundary, are constantly changing.

9. Geduld, p. 6.

10. Geduld, pp. 37–38.

11. Branagh, p. 111.

12. Branagh, p. 12.

13. Branagh, p. 74.

14. Geduld, p. 42.

15. Geduld, p. 43.

16. Laurence Olivier, *On Acting* (London, 1986), p. 64.

17. Olivier, p. 66.

18. Geduld, pp. 54–55.

19. Branagh, pp. 9–10.

20. Gorman Beauchamp, "*Henry V:* Myth, Movie, Play," *College Literature* 5 (1978), p. 231.

21. Geduld, p. 54.

22. Branagh, p. 105.

23. Chris Fitter, unlike most viewers, faults the film for *not* being bloody enough, in contrast, for example, to Polansky's *Macbeth*. Chris Fitter, "A Tale of Two Branaghs: *Henry V*, Ideology, and the Mekong Agincourt," in *Shakespeare Left and Right*, ed. Ivo Kamps (New York, 1991), pp. 270–71.

24. Branagh, p. 114

25. Branagh, p. 11.

26. See chapter 3 above, p. 121.

27. Davies, p. 38.

28. Geduld, p. 47.

29. There is an enormous and well-known literature about Shakespeare's play. I have referred only to some of the less-extensive literature on the two films. An old-fashioned view of Shakespeare's supposedly single-minded celebration of the "mirror of all Christian princes" is, for the most part, rejected nowadays. It has been replaced in some quarters by a "progressive," or "proletarian" reading, one that argues that Shakespeare subverts the heroic Henry, shows that his heart is with the common people, and that, even if the *text* celebrates (for the Elizabethan censor) this imperialistic king, a proper *production* will bring out a subtext that will convey the correct ideological view of the play. See, for example, the article by Chris Fitter, cited above, note 23. Fitter compares the Branagh film with the darker stage production in which Branagh starred before he made the film. Fitter claims that in the popular film for a wider audience, Branagh sold out to the establishment. My view—and Shakespeare's too, I think—is that both of these extreme readings are too simple. Henry is neither a perfect knight-in-shining-armor to be idolized, nor an imperialist impostor to be rejected. Politics is a very complicated business, and it is unlikely that there can ever be a perfect king or a regime that governs erratic human beings with perfect justice. The play is interesting precisely because it suggests that the *very same traits* that make Henry an effective leader are ones that do—and should—give us pause.

30. Marsha McCready, "*Henry V: Onstage* and On Film," *Literature Film Quarterly 5*, no. 4 (1977), p. 317.

31. Robert Heilman makes this observation in an exhortation to teachers of literature not to substitute on a regular basis electronic versions of books for the original printed versions. He argues for the critical distance that the reader of books can maintain, precisely because the written word is less capable of conveying the full sensual immediacy that realistic films can. I suggest that plays staged in the wooden O are between books and movies in this respect. See Robert Heilman, "The Full Man and the Fullness Thereof: Printed Page Versus Sound and Light," in *The Ghost on the Ramparts and Other Essays in the Humanities* (Athens, Ga., 1973), pp. 32–39.

32. For an exception, see the first scene of the BBC *Tempest,* in which one can barely make out a word of what is being said.

33. On theaters as freestanding civic monuments, as opposed to theaters in secluded invisible courtyards, on the one hand, or as facades in modern commercial rows, on the other, see Marvin Carlson, *Places of Performance* (Ithaca, 1989).

34. Andrew Gurr says the adult companies in the open playhouses never had onstage stools for important patrons, though the boy companies and later productions in the Blackfriars Theater did. See *Playgoing in Shakespeare's London* (Cambridge, 1987), p. 30. Olivier's anachronism does contribute to his emphasis on a stratified community. Perhaps it even expresses the romantic nostalgia of a more democratic time for one in which everyone knew his place.

35. See chapter 2, above.

36. Gurr, p. 114.

37. For a historical survey of the way in which the interior arrangement of theaters reflects the aim of exhibiting the spectators to each other, see Carlson, chap. 5.

38. Interestingly, one sometimes still hears applause at the end of a film shown in a college auditorium or as a benefit to raise money among people supporting some political cause. This is a sign that the audience already constitutes a community that responds as a whole.

39. Directed by Giuseppe Tornatore, 1989. A fine depiction of the place of the movie theater in the life of an isolated Italian town before the Second World War.

40. For some similar observations about the differences between seeing films at the movies and watching them at home on VCR, see Vincent Canby, "Is Technology Writing Finis To Joys of the Movie House?" *The New York Times,* January 8, 1984, p. H 17, and "Those VCR's Are Causing Something Momentous," *The New York Times,* December 1, 1985, p. H 19.

41. As this book goes to press, the media are full of reports about the latest progress in the world of video technology: the interactive video. In this new art form, the viewers, now "players," are literally part of the play, they control the action (at this point, consisting mostly of killing, without getting

killed in return). "Now we're violating the most fundamental artifice of cinema: We're constantly breaking the fourth wall. The characters are talking to the audience. I tell the actors, 'The camera is the other actor in the scene. Make your eye contact. Play the scene to the machine.' " John Tierney, "Movies That Push Buttons," *The New York Times*, October 3, 1993, p. H 26.

Index

About the Author

Mera J. Flaumenhaft has taught at St. John's College in Annapolis, Maryland, since 1977. She is the author of essays on Shakespeare, Homer, and Mark Twain, and has translated Machiavelli's *Mandragola*.